ACCLAIM FOR OVERC
CRISIS: 33 COPARENT

"Whether the issue is called alien. ...y this family situation is a crisis c... ...passion and good advice. Authors Moran, McCall, and Sullivan draw on decades of professional experience with families who experience crises in parenting relationships to provide empathy and sound counsel. By examining the problem, exploring solutions, and offering strategies to parents, *Overcoming the Alienation Crisis* explains all aspects of this family dynamic, including how and why this critical problem must be managed, and why court systems today are ill-equipped to provide solutions."

—Annette T. Burns, J.D., Phoenix, Arizona; past President, Association of Family and Conciliation Courts

"*Overcoming the Alienation Crisis: 33 Coparenting Solutions* is an informative and exquisitely practical guidebook, and companion to *Overcoming the Coparenting Trap*, both designed to assist family justice professionals and parents experiencing high-conflict coparenting and parent-child contact problems. Part One provides a cogent framework for parents to understand conflict dynamics and resist–refuse problems and serves as key educational scaffolding to promote change and healing. Parts Two and Three elucidate extremely hands-on solutions to frequently occurring parenting and coparenting dilemmas. Both handbooks are indispensable resources for professionals and parents as they work toward resolving conflicts, improving overall child adjustment, repairing parent-child relationships, and augmenting parenting and coparenting functioning. I use the first handbook routinely with parents towards resolving parenting challenges, coparenting conflicts and parent-child contact problems. I am certain this new publication will be another staple in my practitioner toolkit!"

—Barbara Jo Fidler, Ph.D., co-author of *Children Who Resist Post-Separation Parental Contact: A Differential Approach for Legal and Mental Health Professionals*

"Impressive! A very useful resource for parents dealing with a child's resistance to seeing a parent after a separation or divorce. This contains a thorough analysis of this growing problem, followed by a detailed set of suggestions (33!) on how to handle all of the predictable problems step-by-step. Professionals and parents will benefit from reading this book—and keeping it handy!"

—Bill Eddy, lawyer, therapist, developer of the *New Ways for Families® and author of Don't Alienate the Kids: Raising Resilient Children While Avoiding High Conflict Divorce, 2nd Edition*

"*Overcoming the Alienation Crisis* is one of the most helpful books for professionals and parents in the field of Resist Refuse Parenting Problems. The authors, psychologists who have been in the forefront of thinking about these complex problems, present a research-based, comprehensive and balanced view of this issue. You will certainly want to read how the Dementors contribute to these parent child problems, yet it is the specific and practical solutions, strategies and tips that will help parents move from an escalated coparent to an effective neutral coparent. If you are a professional or parent dealing with these problems, I suggest you read this book NOW."

—Robin M. Deutsch, Ph.D., ABPP;Professor of Clinical Psychology, William James College

"*Overcoming the Alienation Crisis* is a must-read and an essential tool for those working with families in which a child resists or refuses to spend time with a parent. The book is written for multiple audiences while being based upon sound theory and the available research. This rich volume presents evidence-informed practical tools for clinicians, forensic experts, and parents. Clinicians and forensic experts will find that authors Moran, McCall, and Sullivan have made significant contributions to the standard of care for working with this population. The largest audience to benefit from this addition to their toolbox are the families themselves. The prediction and hope is that this book will assist in turning the Alienation Crisis manifesting in Resist Refuse Parenting Problems into an opportunity for change."

—Leslie M. Drozd, Ph.D., co-editor,*Parenting Plan Evaluations: Applied Research for the Family Court*

OVERCOMING THE ALIENATION CRISIS: 33 COPARENTING SOLUTIONS

OTHER BOOKS ABOUT OVERCOMING BARRIERS' WORK

Overcoming the Coparenting Trap: Essential Parenting Skills When a Child Resists a Parent by John A. Moran, PhD; Tyler Sullivan and Matthew Sullivan, PhD

Overcoming Parent-Child Contact Problems: Family-Based Interventions for Resistance, Rejection, and Alienation, Abigail M. Judge, PhD; and Robin M. Deutsch, PhD; editors (New York: Oxford University Press, 2017)

ABOUT OVERCOMING BARRIERS, INC.

Overcoming Barriers is a 501 (c)(3) organization that developed and utilizes the OCB approach to address the issues that arise in high-conflict divorces in which a child is resisting or refusing to see a parent. It continues its mission by providing evidence-informed approaches through:

- Professional development, consultation, and training
- Effective and accessible family centered programs
- Education to advance the field of knowledge
- Awareness of innovative approaches for these families

OVERCOMING THE ALIENATION CRISIS:

33 COPARENTING SOLUTIONS

John A. Moran, PhD
Shawn McCall, PsyD, Esq
Matthew Sullivan, PhD

OVERCOMING BARRIERS, INC.

overcomingbarriers.org
overcomingbarriers@gmail.com

LIMITATIONS

Overcoming Barriers, Inc. and the authors do not warrant that the information herein is complete or applicable to every family navigating divorce with children, and we do not assume and hereby disclaim any liability to any person for any loss or damage caused by errors, inaccuracies, or omissions that may appear in this book.

The information in this book should not be used as a substitute for therapeutic services from mental health professionals. This book does not provide legal opinions nor legal advice and is not intended to serve as a substitute for the advice of licensed professionals.

The authors offer information but are not engaging in rendering mental health, legal, or other professional services through this book. Readers are solely responsible for determining how material in this book applies to their situation.

COVER AND GRAPHIC DESIGN:

Carlos Castro and Alexei Quintero
alexeiquintero.com

ISBN 978-1-7350994-0-8

ACKNOWLEDGMENTS

The authors are grateful to Carole Blane, Executive Director of Overcoming Barriers, Inc. (OCB). Since 2008, Carole has facilitated innumerable conversations among the professionals involved with OCB that provided the crucible in which the ideas in this book evolved.

Our respect and thanks go to Diane Owens whose generous contributions as editor were invaluable to each phase of this book's development. Her keen eye for detail, sensitivity to the sound of the written word, and writing skills made the ideas in the book accessible to both a professional and broader audience.

Finally, the authors express their sincere appreciation to the families who sought our assistance and enabled us to better understand the service needs of families in an alienation crisis.

CONTENTS

PART III
Coparenting Tools and Strategies

*Note: When a child resists or refuses contact with a parent, in this book we refer to it as "Resist Refuse Problems." Other terms for parent-child contact problems are listed in Chapter 1.

PART ONE: THE ALIENATION CRISIS

The etymology (word origin) of "crisis":

1. From the Latinized form of Greek *krisis*: "Turning point in a disease" that could lead to death or recovery.
2. Early 15th century: "Vitally important or decisive state of things, the point at which change must come for better or worse."

INTRODUCTION

You may have picked up this book on the recommendation of your therapist or attorney. At this point, you are likely sick and tired of coparenting with someone you see as the problem—someone you believe deserves very little or no parenting time. Each uncomfortable interaction with your coparent seems more troubling and stressful than the last. Perhaps the conflict has even reached the point that your child is now resisting or refusing contact with you or the other parent, and your family is now in a crisis.

Did you pick up this book because you are searching for a way forward that will bring some relief from the conflict and even peace—if you dare hope for that? You are not alone in searching for a solution. This is a crisis that has confounded professionals and the courts.

This book offers information and practical approaches to help you and your coparent restore coparenting coordination and cooperation. We want to help you remove your children from the crosshairs of your continual conflict. We want to help you for the sake of your children.

We are three psychologists who together have many decades of experience working with high-conflict parents. We regularly write professional articles and make presentations at conferences for counselors, attorneys, and judges about high-conflict coparenting problems including alienation, domestic violence, and parents with mental health conditions.

We know from experience that coparenting is never easy, even in the best of circumstances. We also know that splitting up one household with children into two separate households is guaranteed to require some adjustments for both parents and children. Children challenge even the most skillful coparents. They will leave important stuff at the other parent's house. They may do what children in intact families do and pit one parent against the other using such common tactics as, "But Dad lets me do that!" They may even embellish or hide the truth about life with the other parent. Kids will be kids.

When a child resists or refuses contact with a parent without a reasonable explanation, the family goes into crisis. The resisted parent is alarmed; the favored parent is alarmed. Accusations, blame, and threats fly back and forth between parents. The child becomes distressed, if not traumatized. Polarized and often exaggerated explanations emerge to explain what is going on. Coparenting breaks down. Parents are also unable to agree on an explanation for the child's resistance. Is it caused by poor quality parenting, alienation, the child's exposure to domestic violence, or something else? Typically, coparents end up pitted against each other in a bitter dispute that involves extended family and legal advocates supporting one parent against the other. The peaceful, safe family nest the parents wanted to create is self-destructing at enormous costs for all.

Family members find themselves in a predicament with no easy escape but involving lots of difficult choices. For example, should a coparent insist a child spend time with the resisted parent, even though the child may be anxious and fearful or potentially act out? Should a parent call the police when the coparent does not bring the child to a court-ordered custody exchange, even though the child may witness the police confronting a parent?

With an alienation crisis, both parents are confronted with moral and legal dilemmas. For example, a parent may believe in complying with court orders, but also that the child should be able to choose, even though doing so violates a court order. The dilemma may be between the principles of justice and mercy. Should a parent argue about the unfairness of a situation, or should a parent focus on being compassionate and forgiving their coparent for their hurtful behavior?

A parent may have to choose between a short-term priority—protecting a child from the stress of a reunification intervention, for example—versus a long-term priority such as strengthening the child's ability to cope with difficult relationships. Children also get caught in dilemmas, like being honest versus being loyal. For example, when a child returns from parenting time, should they talk about the fun time spent with the other parent, or should they act as if the entire experience with the other parent was awful?

Saving the Family Tree from a Branch Shredder

Coparents want to resolve the alienation crisis as quickly as possible. Given the huge amount of information available online, it is not hard to find support for their side of the argument. But a one-sided approach to a family problem is rarely effective and usually drives the family toward a court battle. Parents often get caught up in fighting, but the critical issue is what needs to be done to protect the child from the psychological damage of an extended battle.

Most parents who ask family court to resolve a resist-refuse problem are disappointed by the outcome. The courts rarely find either parent solely responsible for the problem. Likewise, the courts rarely award exclusive care and control of the child to one parent even when findings are made in one parent's favor. When the courts are involved in these cases, a parent's efforts to protect the child may backfire. The court may order punitive consequences if it finds that a parent is engaging in alienation or restrictive gatekeeping. The court might even change legal custody or the child's primary residence.

Our experience has been two-fold. When all is said and done, we have found that generally (1) after hefty resources are spent, the courts find it is in the child's best interest to have a relationship with both parents; and (2) the courts will order the family into reunification therapy that offers skills development suggestions similar to those described in this book. Although trust between you and your coparent may be low and anger high, it is usually better to work together on the parent-child contact problem. Time is the enemy of any malignancy, and an intensifying parent-child contact problem is a family malignancy. Implementing the corrective strategies and tools suggested in this book may be stressful for all family members, including the child. In most situations, providing skillful, unified coparenting support for the child is far better than eliminating a parent from the child's life or subjecting the family to ongoing court battles.

Why Read This Book?

Simply put, an alienation crisis is a malignancy for any family. The parent-child contact problem must be managed. Going to court is what you do when you're down to nothing but bad choices.

Our central concern is the emotional damage to children that accumulate from parent-child contact problems. Of course, parents worry about their child and want the parent-child contact problem to end. We hope this book helps parents to better understand and navigate the painful choices that confront the family in the wake of refusal, alienation, and justified rejection.

Chapters 2, 3, and 4 describe types and causes of parent-child contact problems. Parental alienation grabs the headlines, but understanding what is going on with a child who resists or refuses contact with a parent requires looking at many contributing factors. Understanding is more than just asking whether the children have been alienated (the fault of the favored parent) or estranged (the fault of the resisted parent).

Chapters 5 through 8 look at conflict escalation as the common denominator among families that develop an alienation crisis. Escalated coparenting conflict leads to communication breaking down and the children being trapped in loyalty conflicts. When the children are allowed to manage their divided feelings by significantly reducing or refusing contact with a parent, the parents often turn to third parties for assistance with opposing agendas. Behavioral health professionals, attorneys, police, child protective services, and others are enlisted to help the family. Too often such services are unable to contain and reverse the growing animosity among family members. Sometimes, legal and mental health professionals make it worse. Family members are trapped in polarized thinking, blame, and bitter resentment about the conflict they have had to endure. Coparenting as a leadership function for the family fails. Efforts to resolve the parent-child problem reach a stalemate, and the court is asked to make decisions that usually cannot remedy parental disputes and decision-making failures. However, the courts often order family therapy to correct faulty dynamics within the family and to restore coparenting cooperation that will lead to family peace and healthy relationships.

In Part Two, we offer 33 Solutions for Frequently Encountered Coparenting Problems. Solutions are presented in a Q&A format and include the following areas:

- Improving your coparenting communication
- Responding to your child's complaints
- Responding to your child's resistance
- Talking to your child about their other parent
- Supporting your anxious child.

In Part Three, Chapters 14 through 17 describe coparenting tools and strategies. We discuss parallel coparenting, a model for disengaged coparenting that minimizes coparenting contact and opportunities for conflict. We explain five shifts that parents can make to reduce conflict and restore family harmony. We also address how to reduce the resentment parents and children carry after the active phases of the conflict end. In the final chapter, we look at what makes family therapy more or less likely to succeed.

INTRODUCTION: KEY POINTS

- Parents often get caught up in fighting about who is to blame, but the critical issue is what needs to be done to protect the child from the psychological damage of an extended battle.
- Working together on the parent-child contact problem is the best strategy, in spite of your anger and lack of trust.
- An alienation crisis is a malignancy for any family. The parent-child contact problem must be managed.
- Understanding what is going on with a child who resists or refuses contact with a parent requires looking at many contributing factors. Understanding is more than just asking whether the child has been alienated (the fault of the favored parent) or estranged (the fault of the resisted parent).

CHAPTER 1

Types of Resist Refuse Problems

TYPES OF RESIST REFUSE PROBLEMS

When a child resists or refuses contact with one of their parents, we call this Resist Refuse Problems. Throughout this book we shorten the term to RRP.

Terms commonly used by behavioral health professionals to refer to RRP[1] include parent-child contact problems, parental alienation syndrome,[2] parental alienation,[3] strained parent-child relationships,[4] restrictive gatekeeping,[5] alienated child,[6] and pathological alienation.[7] These terms apply when the child's affection is alienated from a parent. In this book, we simply use the term "alienation."

Children's adjustment to divorce and separation can result in different degrees of closeness to each parent.[8] We refer to the parent whom the child prefers as "the favored parent," and the parent whom the child resists or refuses contact as "the resisted parent."

The pyramid in Figure 1.1 shows different types of parent-child relationships among divorced families.

At the top of the pyramid in figure 1, children have a strong, secure attachment to both parents—clearly the ideal family relationship situation. Ask children from these families what parenting time schedule they want, and they will say, "Equal time with Mom and with Dad. That's fair."

Going down the pyramid, children often develop an *affinity* to one parent. A child's affinity to a parent means they feel more comfortable with a parent. The affinity may be based on any number of factors: the child's age, temperament, gender, or an interest they share with the parent such as music, sports, or religious practices. A child might prefer the parenting style of one parent. An affinity might be based on the amount of time a child has spent with a parent in the past. For example, if Mom was at home while Dad was at work, the child may say that since they were little they felt closer to Mom. A child having an affinity for one parent is common and healthy, and often shifts over time. For example, a preteen boy who has lived primarily with his mother might want to experience what it would be like to live with Dad for a while. Usually a child with an affinity to one parent does not strongly protest the parenting time arrangement.

Figure 1: Different types of parent-child relationships among divorced families

STRONG ATTACHMENT TO BOTH PARENTS

AFFINITY: MILD PREFERENCE FOR ONE PARENT

ALLIGNMENT: STRONG PREFERENCE FOR ONE PARENT; CONTACT CONTINUES WITH OTHER PARENT

JUSTIFIED REJECTION — HYBRID — ALIENATION

Justified rejection: Due to partner violence, emotional or other abuse, inept parenting

Hybrid: A combination of alienation and justified rejection

Alienation: Unjustified resistance or rejection of a parent

More problematic are *alignments* that develop between a child and one of their parents. When a child aligns with a parent, they may express in strong and rigid terms their wish to spend more time with the favored parent. After divorce, a child's alignment may be caused by a loyalty conflict. In response to on-going conflict, the child may side with the parent they are most comfortable with. When the child chooses a side, they can stop wondering about which parent is "right" and which parent is "wrong." If they are allowed to choose a side and refuse contact with the other parent, the child is relieved of the burden of going between embattled households and the burden of talking about one parent in front of the other, which is usually awkward. Continuing down the pyramid, when a child resists or refuses contact with a parent, an important distinction is made between *justified rejection* and *alienation*.

A child's resistance may be justified in resisting a parent if that parent has been largely absent from the child's life, physically violent or emotionally abusive, or if the parent has a substance use disorder or some form of mental illness that has impacted their parenting. A child's resistance may be justified because the parent has a new partner or has relocated, depending on the impact of those changes on the child. Significant parenting skills limitations could be a reasonable basis for a child's resistance. For example, the parent regularly uses a loud voice and harsh language to discipline the child. Or, a parent puts a lot of pressure on a child to be responsible with schoolwork and home chores, without also providing a warm and fun-filled home environment.

More often than not, the Resist Refuse Problem is most accurately described as a *hybrid* of justified resistance and alienation. That is, the behavior of the resisted parent strained their relationship with the child, but also the favored parent engaged in alienating behaviors. Usually there is heated disagreement between the parents about who did how much of what.

CHAPTER 1: KEY POINTS

- Children's adjustment to divorce and separation can result in different degrees of closeness to each parent. This is normal.
- As the coparenting conflict escalates, the child feels increasing pressure to align with the favored parent, and sometimes they will completely reject the other parent.
- More often than not, custody evaluators conclude that the parent-child contact problem is most accurately described as a *hybrid* of justified resistance and alienation.

CHAPTER 2

Alienation

ALIENATION

Alienation occurs when a child has previously had a reasonably good relationship with a parent, and the reasons the child states for resisting the parent are unjustified or unreasonable, given the parent's behavior or relationship history with the child. As we will discuss shortly, the cause of the alienation crisis is usually a complex pattern of interactions among many people over time, not simply the alienating behavior of a parent. It is quite rare that a single factor is responsible for a child's resistance. Alienation is one of the most complicated family relationship problems that legal and mental health professionals face in their practices. The child's resistance stems from multiple factors interacting over time that ultimately impact the child. When a child is alienated from a parent, the parent-child relationship needs to be preserved, or the child will be harmed.

The number of families dealing with allegations of alienation in the courts has increased in the last ten years.[9] Figure 2 shows the increase in U.S. court cases in which the court ruled alienation had occurred.[10]

What accounts for this increase? More children spending their time in two households provides fertile ground for coparenting conflict.

Figure 2: Number of Cases Where PA Found in U.S. Courts 1985-2018

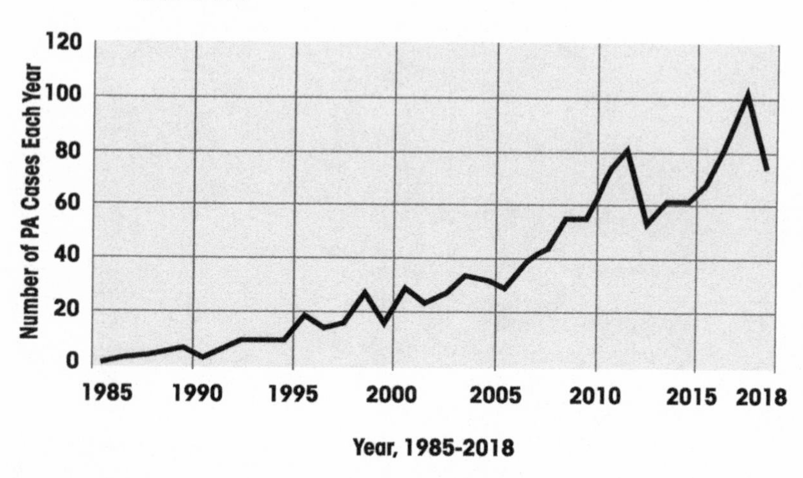

Roughly 15 percent of parents who share custody are characterized as high conflict (more on this in later chapters). When coparents are struggling with their relationship, and the issue of a child's preference for one parent comes up, conflict can quickly escalate. If one parent thinks the child is not comfortable or safe with the other parent, and the other parent thinks their coparent is undermining their relationship with the child, the conflict can go nuclear. Later, we will describe in detail how escalating coparenting conflict can become a black hole in which the family's previously shared affections and mutual respect disappear—never to be seen again.

Alienation can be alleged about a parent, both reasonably and as a malicious strategy to gain an advantage in one's custody case. Regardless, focusing on blame and alleging that alienation is solely the cause of the child's resistance fails to address the multiple factors responsible for a child's rejection of a parent. Each parent typically denies their contribution and places exclusive blame for the problem on the other parent. Often, there is reliable evidence of each parent's contribution.

Another source of increased accusations of alienation in court cases is the explosion of information about parental alienation available on the internet. Family law professionals who specialize in working with alienation cringe when a client reports that based on their extensive internet research, they have determined they are the victims of parental alienation. Although the client may be a victim of the other parent's campaign of hate to destroy their relationship with their child, cases of "pure" alienation are rare. Usually allegations of alienation are too simple an answer for a complicated problem. We appreciate that for a parent suffering the loss of a relationship with their child, a horrible force seems to be at work, and alienation fits the bill. But in families with moderate to severe RRP, a predictable result of the severe distress that comes with RRP is that both parents and the child end up with oversimplified explanations about what is going on. The favored parent is convinced why the child is resisting—the coparent deserves it. The resisted parent is convinced that the child is resisting them because their relationship with the child is being undermined through alienating behaviors. The resisted parent may even conclude that the child has been brainwashed. With both parents in deep hurt and fear, they may turn to online support groups that provide one-sided and sometimes misleading information that supports their views.

In 1986, Richard Gardner, MD, brought widespread attention to the problem of parental alienation syndrome. Since then, our understanding of alienation has advanced quite a bit. As we saw in the last chapter, alienation is now identified as one of several types of RRP, and specialized interventions have been developed for families with different kinds of RRP. Here are some reliable findings from 30-plus years of social science research into alienation:

1. Alienation is a real phenomenon. Social science research has repeatedly shown harmful effects to children's psychological development when alienation persists.
2. Parental Alienation Syndrome (PAS), a 1980s approach to understanding severe alienation, has significant flaws. PAS should not be used to describe RRP. However, calling parental alienation "junk science" is throwing the baby out with the bathwater.
3. Domestic violence, child abuse, and alienation are real and can coexist in families. Often, the argument about the cause of the child's resistance is presented as alienation versus domestic violence. The polarization is made worse by the gender-related nature of each issue. That is, mothers are often the victims of domestic violence (although fathers are also victims of domestic violence). And, fathers are often the victims of alienation (although mothers are victims of alienation too). The polarization is made worse by court battles in which lawyers vehemently argue their client's position.

4. The focus of the court should be what is best for the child. The court first needs to determine if the child having a full and meaningful relationship with both parents is in the child's best interests. If so, the court's determination of the factors that contributed to RRP in the family can help to organize the behavioral health intervention to serve the best interests of the child.

Alienation is a family issue. It arises in response to the behavior of family members, extended family, family friends and experts called in to help the family. Resolving RRP requires positive contributions from as many individuals inside and outside the family as possible. Improving the coparents' ability to communicate and negotiate a plan of action is essential to resolve RRP. Social science research repeatedly finds that ongoing coparenting conflict harms children—not divorce per se, but the conflict itself. And the coparents' inability to agree to and implement a plan of action can be an insurmountable obstacle to resolving RRP.

CHAPTER 2: KEY POINTS

- Alienation occurs when a child has previously had a reasonably good relationship with a parent, and the reasons the child states for resisting the parent are unjustified or unreasonable, given the parent's behavior or relationship history with the child.
- The cause of the alienation crisis is usually a complex pattern of interactions among many people over time, not simply the alienating behavior of one parent.
- Usually allegations of alienation are too simple an answer for a complicated problem.
- Domestic violence, child abuse, and alienation are real and can coexist in families.
- Alienation is a family issue. It arises in response to the behavior of family members, extended family, family friends, and experts called in to help the family.

CHAPTER 3

What Causes Resist Refuse Problems?

WHAT CAUSES RESIST REFUSE PROBLEMS?

Parents searching for solutions to RRP almost always conclude that the root cause of the problem is that their coparent has a personality problem, most often the narcissistic, borderline, or antisocial/psychopathic type; or a mental condition such as Bipolar Disorder or Major Depressive Disorder. The parent then reasons that because their coparent has one of these problems, the solution is to severely restrict or suspend the contact between that parent and the child until evaluation and successful treatment of the deficient parent occurs.

There is data to support this line of thinking. Research suggests that in about 12 to 18 percent of families with intractable coparenting conflict (as we will see later, "intractable" coparenting conflict persists, in spite of multiple efforts to reduce it), one or both parents has a significant personality disorder.[11] Bill Eddy, LCSW, has written extensively about how individuals with "high-conflict personalities" can be difficult to deal with—whether in the family, at work, or when involved in a legal and mental health context.[12]

An obstacle to conflict de-escalation is that parents are too liberal in applying the label of personality disorder. When behavioral health professionals who specialize in family court cases communicate their findings to the court, they hesitate to assign personality diagnoses to parents. They hesitate for many reasons, but especially because the personality disorder diagnosis can be given too much weight. The coparent will use the personality disorder diagnosis as a "label to disable," that is, to repeatedly hammer the theme that the coparent has been identified with a personality disorder and should therefore be deprived of parenting time and/or legal decision making-authority. They assume the diagnosis of a personality disorder is a "smoking gun," that is, irrefutable and definitive proof that the coparent is unfit, and the court should act to restrict his or her right to parent. However, personality pathology, which occurs on a continuum, may or may not be relevant to their capacity to parent. A parent may have a personality dysfunction that has little impact on the child. The critical issue is the quality of the interactions between the parent and child. For example, if a parent is narcissistic and prone to getting caught up in their own thinking and missing emotional cues, this is not much of a problem when the child is an infant, although it may become more problematic later with a preteen.

And there is another important reason to go easy on personality disorder assumptions. To protect the children, the coparents need to override their tendency to focus on the flaws of the coparent. Rather, they need to work around triggers that exacerbate personality problems, and as best they can, support the coparent in implementation of the court-ordered parenting plan. But asking a coparent embroiled in intractable family conflict not to focus on the personality flaws of the other coparent is like saying, "Don't think about an elephant."

It is beyond dispute that parental problems, such as personality disorders, often have an adverse impact on children. We do not wish to underestimate at all how important it is to protect children, and how a parent with a personality disorder can threaten the best interests of the child. However, in the families we work with, coparents focusing on one another's personality and parenting skills deficits does not reduce the conflict or RRP. Quite the opposite! This blame-focus maintains the most pathological aspect of the family dynamic.

The truth is, there is plenty of blame to go around. Each family member has contributed to the parent-child problem in one way or another and must make changes to resolve it. Ironically, parents who focus on placing blame, often get blamed and accused of sounding like a victim. Their blame statements suggest that they take little responsibility for what happened and have no role in solving their child's problems. A favored parent might say, "His problem with the kids is his problem. It's not my responsibility to fix it." It can be difficult to stop blaming and give up the victim identity; victims know who they are—a person who was wronged.[13] Also, the strength of self-righteous anger that comes from being a victim creates more problems.

In the end, children will place blame on both parents. The children didn't want a divorce, and if they had to go through it, they wanted the kind where the kids go back and forth, and there's no big conflict between their parents. Older teens who are getting ready to leave home can't wait to get out of the house and away from the divorce conflict craziness. During an intervention, a 15-year-old who had stonewalled her dad for two years blurted out, "I don't need either of my parents!" The teaching seems to be that while intractable RRP is being played out, the children are keeping their deeper thoughts to themselves. Often those thoughts are along the lines of: "It's not my divorce! I wish my parents would be mature enough to figure it out and keep me out of it."

So, it is an oversimplification to say that RRP is caused solely by a parent's personality disorder. In the 30-plus years that professionals have studied alienation-type problems, they have identified multiple factors that can contribute to RRP.

Multiple Interrelated Causes of RRP

Since Richard Gardner put alienation on professionals' radar, there has been a lot of discussion about types and causes of RRP. Figure 3 shows causes identified by psychologists as contributing to RRP. There is a lot of information in the figure, so we discuss the factors in groups: 1) characteristics of the child; 2) parents' personalities and parenting styles; 3) the coparenting relationship; 4) the role of siblings and extended family; 5) the courts and litigation; and 6) the role of behavioral health professionals. Finally, we discuss the cycle of conflict—how conflict in the family leads to resistance and more conflict.

Figure 3: Multiple Factors Contributing to Resist Refuse Problems

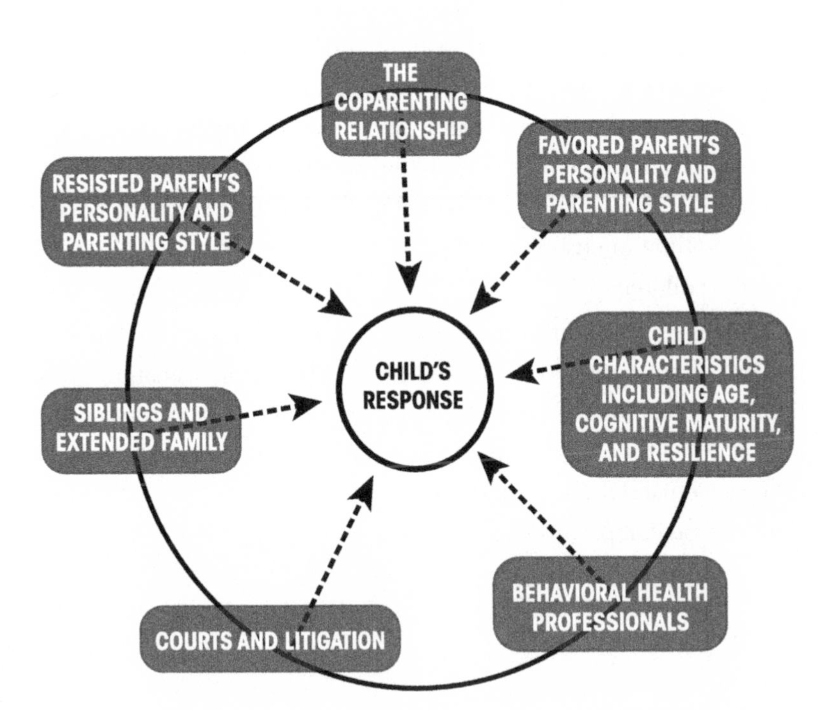

Adapted from Kelly & Johnston, 2001

1. Child Characteristics Including Age, Cognitive Maturity, and Resilience

In general, preteen and teenage children are more vulnerable to alienation. Children who are less socially and emotionally mature, or have special developmental needs appear to be more vulnerable to RRP. For example, a child with an anxiety disorder may be more reactive to parental conflict and more likely to side with a parent to minimize their anxious feelings. A child with a health problem may unrealistically resist being away from a parent who provided a large majority of their medical care, especially if a dispute develops between the parents about what kind of medical care is necessary.

2. Parents' Personalities and Parenting Styles

As noted in Chapter 2, alienation exists only when the resisted parent had a good relationship with the child prior to the onset of the child's resistance and/or rejection of that parent. Many factors go into making a good relationship between a child and a parent. Primary among these is the parent's involvement in multiple aspects of the child's life. Some divorce experts maintain that a parent requires at least 30 percent of the parenting time to ensure that they have fully meaningful involvement with the children.[14]

In families with RRP, though not universal, it is not unusual for one or both of the parents to have problematic behavior or parenting styles. Sometimes parents do not have significant personality issues or problematic parenting styles during the marriage. However, in response to the stress of separation and divorce—and especially the stress of RRP—parenting skills can be compromised.

Favored parents may be:[15]

- Overly protective
- Anxious/enmeshed
- Emotionally dysregulated
- Vengeful/furious

Resisted parents may be:

- The minimally involved or absent parent
- The harsh punitive parent
- Low in emotional responsiveness
- High in demands for maturity
- The angry-rigid/blaming parent

3. The Coparenting Relationship

The relationship between the parents, both prior to and following separation, is key to the child making a successful transition to living between two households. Prior to the separation, one parent may restrict the other parent's access to the children, especially when the specter of divorce looms large. If the children are exposed to frequent arguments, domestic violence, or emotional abuse between the parents while they are living together, after the separation, the children may be ripe for aligning against the parent they viewed as the aggressor. However, sometimes the children align with the aggressor, despite how counterintuitive this may seem.

Following the parents' separation, the parents' support of each other's relationship with the child is critical to the type of relationship the child develops with each of them. Perhaps our biggest takeaway message is that coparenting conflict often leads parents into tragically misguided judgments about how to support the child's relationship with their other parent.

4. The Role of Siblings and Extended Family

Children's responses to their parents' separation differ, depending on the age of the child. Using the example from above, a teenage daughter may much more forcefully reject a dad who leaves for an affair than a younger sibling would. The older sibling may be less inhibited in complaining about a dad's new relationship. Or, if an older sibling refuses to follow the court-ordered parenting time schedule, a younger sibling may think that they shouldn't be required to follow it either.

Following separation, the extended family often offers support to the parents and children that may contribute to RRP. Their support may include taking over some childcare duties. This can put the extended family member in a position in which they are tempted to talk to the children about the divorce. It is not unusual for extended family members to help with divorce-related expenses, including litigation costs.

5. The Role of the Courts and Litigation

Most parents want to stay out of court. Judges encourage use of counseling and alternative dispute resolution processes, such as mediation, arbitration, and parenting coordinators. From our perspective, the best family court attorneys advocate for their clients and avoid bringing disputes into court, except as a last resort. But when a child rejects parenting time with a parent, or when major elements of the parenting plan are being ignored, it becomes necessary for the resisted parent to ask for court intervention to have the opportunity to restore their relationship with the resisting child. The large amount of the family's financial resources consumed by court intervention contributes substantially to the resentment parents feel toward each other. But court involvement can also contribute to the resentment the child feels toward the resisted parent.

The child will know if the parents are going to court to fight over time with them. A substantial body of research shows that children feel the stress of divorce more when parents are fighting over parenting time.[16] The resisting child resents the resisted parent for subjecting them and the favored parent to the stress of court, which exacerbates their rejection of that parent. The child may demand an explanation from the resisted parent about why they "took us to court," referring to the child and the favored parent. The resisted parent is in a pickle. On the one hand, they are prohibited from sharing information about the divorce, so they cannot say what their rationale was. On the other hand, since the child holds deep resentment about the stress of court on the favored parent and the child, whatever rationale the resisted parent offers may be received with negative bias and discounted.

6. The Role of Behavioral Health Professionals

RRP are among the most complex and difficult family problems to treat. Few therapists have the specialized training necessary to work effectively with RRP. An under-qualified therapist may provide assessment information, treatment recommendations, and therapeutic approaches that make the problem worse.

In our experience, families with RRP in the moderate to severe range go through multiple failed interventions that serve to confirm family members' belief that the situation with the resisted parent is hopeless. And family members can suffer from therapy fatigue. For example, children often complain that they don't want to go to any more therapy.

Cycles of Conflict

"Conflict escalation" is an overarching, fundamental factor that both causes conflict and makes it worse. It is a common denominator for RRP. In a healthy divorce, conflict is contained. In an unhealthy divorce, conflict grinds on and escalates, which sets off chain reactions of conflict. For example, Mom's attorney files a motion stating that Dad "has an anger management problem that makes him unfit to parent." In response, Dad's attorney makes a similarly nasty allegation about Mom. The next time the parents exchange the children, they bristle with hostility. Following the exchange, the children either withdraw or act out. One sibling tells Mom that Dad got really mad at another sibling, and on and on. Insults, hurt, and feelings of being unjustly treated pile up.

Anger and resentment build with repeated episodes of escalated conflict. Coparents feel a powerful resistance toward interacting with each other. Their resistance toward each other provides fertile ground for a child's resistance toward the resisted parent to grow. The family becomes a tinderbox in which a small slight provokes an escalated reaction. In a nutshell, the conflict becomes a superpower to the parents. It takes over—the parents are no longer in charge of the family. The conflict becomes the defining characteristic of the family and their "divorce from hell." The conflict can make each of the other identified causes of RRP worse—interpersonal arguments are notorious for leading to regrettable behavior.

To the extent that conflict escalation is an underlying cause of RRP, conflict de-escalation and peacemaking are central to restoring a parent-child relationship. They are a principal focus of this book.

Figure 4: Cycles of Conflict

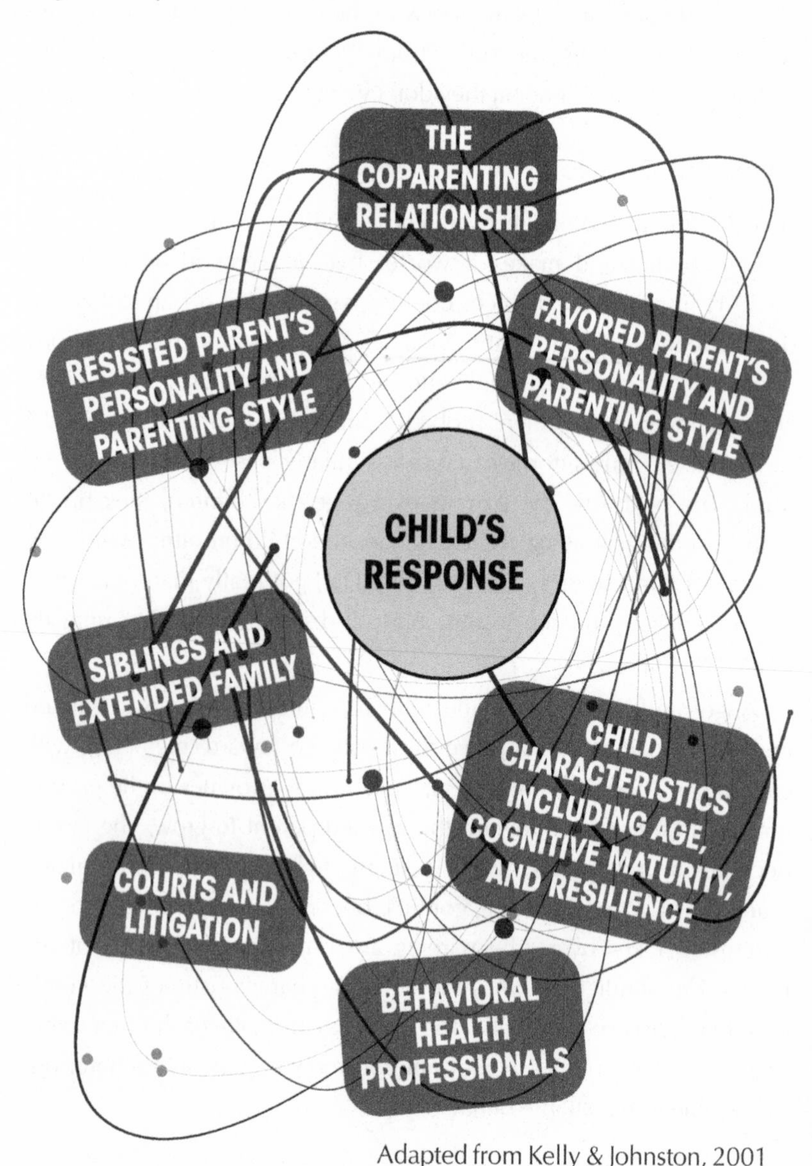

Adapted from Kelly & Johnston, 2001

CHAPTER 3: KEY POINTS

- To protect the children, the coparents need to override their tendency to focus on their coparent's flaws.
- The truth is, there is plenty of blame to go around. Each family member has contributed to the parent-child problem in one way or another, and to one degree or another, must make changes to resolve it.
- Coparenting conflict often leads parents into tragically misguided judgments about how to support the child's relationship with their other parent.
- "Conflict escalation" is an overarching, fundamental factor that both causes conflict and makes it worse. It is a common denominator for RRP.
- Conflict becomes a superpower to the parents. It takes over—the parents are no longer in charge of the family. The conflict becomes the defining characteristic of the family and their "divorce from hell."
- Conflict de-escalation and peacemaking are central to restoring a parent-child relationship.

CHAPTER 4

Children Caught in the Crisis

CHILDREN CAUGHT IN THE CRISIS

Ending an intimate relationship that has produced a child is dreadful. Telling the children the family is breaking up, setting up dual households, restructuring the family finances, and moving into the routines of shared parenting are among life's most difficult challenges.

When the divorce transition goes well, family members can emerge into a surge of growth as they restructure their lives. Parents and children connect more directly. New relationships are developed. Life is rich again and manageable. But the stress of the divorce transition is very real. Both parents and children struggle.

As parents exit what had been their intimate partnership, they go through deep internal changes including disappointment, disorientation, discouragement, disenchantment, disengagement, and disempowerment.[17] There is no shortage of stories about divorcing parents who struggle with anxiety, depression, and other adjustment problems. They often act out their distress with emotional displays in front of the children, have romantic flings, make extravagant purchases, or use substances to cope. The stress of divorce transition can last and last. Twenty-five years after the divorce, some parents still bitterly complain to their adult children about their former spouse.

Children face radical change in their lifestyles—living in different homes, bedrooms, neighborhoods, and family cultures. As the safety net of the intact family shreds, children feel deep insecurity and confusion: Why did the break-up happen? What does it mean? What is going to happen now?

It is hard for parents to know how upset their children are. The children's ability to understand their own reactions is just developing, and parents are more self-focused. Children often don't have the words or concepts to express what they are feeling. And, children use denial as their first line of defense against divorce—they often avoid thinking or talking about their anxious feelings and confusion. This is why counseling to assist children with divorce is sometimes unproductive;

the children may not want to talk or think about it. Their lack of readiness to communicate may mean that the divorce is ripping them up without the parents knowing.

How Can Divorce Harm Children?

Most children are resilient and after an initial transition period successfully adjust to the stressors of divorce. How well children cope with divorce depends on a lot of different factors such as:

- The quality of parenting the children receive from each parent
- The child's age, health, current adjustment, gender and temperament
- The presence or absence of supportive siblings, extended family, and community support
- The family's cultural traditions
- The economic resources of the family

Thousands of studies have examined the impact of divorce on children. Kelly reviewed the social science research on divorce and concluded that the risk of problems for children of divorced parents is more than double (25 percent) than that of children of married parents (10 percent).[18] Research also shows that the risk to children in families with chronic coparenting conflict is even higher, especially when the conflict involves the children.

Children from high-conflict divorce are more likely to:

- Have more relationship problems with peers and authority figures
- Get in trouble for acting-out behaviors such as fighting, lying, or disobedience
- Have lower academic performance or drop out of school
- Become pregnant as adolescents
- Have problems with early onset of cigarette smoking or substance use
- Struggle with depression, anxiety, and lower self-esteem

- Have weaker ties and poorer relationships with their parents
- Have stress-related physical health problems, both during the divorce transition period and across the lifespan

Here are statements by Joan Kelly[19] and Judith Wallerstein,[20] two prominent divorce researchers about the impact of intractable divorce conflict on children:

> "The stress caused by exposure to anger is perhaps the most notable consequence of parental conflict on children. Children as young as 18 months old become emotionally upset when they witness angry exchanges between adults, and by the age of 5 or 6, children's distress is evident in their attempts to intervene in the conflict."

> "Perhaps the most serious effect of parents' quarreling over children is that the kids learn that feelings are too painful; they teach themselves not to feel pleasure or pain. In the battle between you, they learn to be polished diplomats. They'll tell each of you what you want to hear most—not because they're liars but because they want desperately to soothe each of you, to calm you down, to reduce their fears that you'll become enraged. They're afraid of your anger, they pity you, and they want you to feel better [...] Children caught in the flames of a high-conflict divorce have been referred to as 'children of Armageddon'—victims of the final war on earth. They are true casualties. Parents trapped in mutual anger often become heedless of anything else."

When Does Divorce Harm Children?

Divorce itself does not harm children. Most children are resilient to the stress of divorce. Divorce tends to harm children when any combination of six factors are active:[21]

1. High levels of conflict between the parents
2. Domestic violence
3. Poor quality of parenting
4. Poor coparenting relationship
5. Low economic resources
6. Loss of a relationship with one of the parents

RRP usually involves all six factors. Coparenting conflict is always high when children resist or refuse contact with a parent. The favored parent alleges that poor quality parenting, child abuse, and/or domestic violence by the resisted parent is the cause of the child's resistance. The resisted parent alleges that they and their child have been the victims of poor-quality parenting including alienating behavior.

When RRP develops, most families have limited family resources that are further taxed by the expense of litigation. After RRP develops, the children are at risk of losing relationships with the resisted parent and one side of their extended family. Over the long run, they may push back against the favored parent for exposing them to the alienation predicament. Later in life, children may also develop problems with peer relationships.

Unresolved RRP damages children. Children whose adequate parent is erased from their childhood are likely to have behavior or relationship problems in young adulthood. Remember, every child has a part of each parent in them. A central task of the developing child and young adult is to recognize and integrate the good and bad aspects of each of their parents. This fundamental psychological integration does not become less important when parents separate and divorce. When there is no contact with a parent, this essential psychological integration is impaired. What we know is that even though a child's behavior may not immediately reflect the damage of a cut-off relationship, their behavior as an adult will. A favored parent's intent (malicious or not) to protect their child from the rejected parent's negative qualities in the absence of substantiated abuse or domestic violence doesn't do the child any favors in the long run.

Conflict between parents is a defining feature of families with RRP. The effects of divorce conflict on children are usually invisible, slow growing, and hard for parents to detect. Among professionals who work in family court and who see the impact of divorce conflict on children, the consistent cry is for parents to protect children.

A primary goal of this book is to help parents protect children from the malignant effects of divorce conflict. These problems are not hopeless. And even if they don't yield to a total cure, they need to be managed skillfully and with care.

CHAPTER 4: KEY POINTS

- It is hard for parents to know how upset their children are. Children often don't have the words or concepts to express what they are feeling. And, children use denial and avoidance as their first line of defense against divorce—they often avoid thinking or talking about their anxious feelings and confusion.
- Divorce itself does not harm children. Most children are resilient to the stress of divorce.
- The effects of divorce conflict on children are usually invisible, slow growing, and hard for parents to detect.
- Every child has a part of each parent in them. A central task of the developing child and young adult is to recognize and integrate the good and bad aspects of each of their parents.

CHAPTER 5

Intractable Resist Refuse Problems

INTRACTABLE RESIST REFUSE PROBLEMS

Intractable means hard to control or deal with, stubborn, not easily managed, or resolved. For example, someone who suffered a back injury might have intractable pain. A person with depression whose symptoms do not get better with medication and counseling is said to have an intractable depression. Alcoholism often is an intractable problem. Smoking is intractable when multiple attempts to quit fail. Parent-child contact problems are intractable when they persist and worsen, in spite of multiple attempts to resolve them.

Most coparents must overcome hostile and oppositional feelings toward one another following separation and divorce.[22] Eighty percent of parents gradually recover and move on to build fulfilling lives by the sixth year after divorce. Over time, 20 to 25 percent of coparents continue to be engaged in conflict. These coparents have a high-conflict relationship; that is, their coparenting relationship problems are "intractable." Some characteristics of these problems include:

- Parents are unable to implement the parenting plan without recurring conflict.
- Their animosity and lack of trust in one another is so great that they may not communicate essential information to each other about the children.
- They are more likely to involve the police and child protective services.
- They tend to repeatedly return to court, disputing issues including parenting time, legal decision-making, allegations of mental illness or personality disorders, domestic violence, parental alienation, substance abuse, and child maltreatment.
- Either one or both of the parents are likely to have dysfunctional personality traits.

Referring to coparenting conflict or a parent-child contact problem as "intractable" can seem harsh. The term seems to imply the problem is impossible to solve.[23] Perhaps there is a better term such as refractory, stubborn, protracted, complex, gnarly, or gridlocked. However, the important point about intractable problems is that although they are difficult and may not yield to a total "cure," these problems are not hopeless. And, they need to be managed.

Families with intractable parent-child contact problems enter into a world that can seem bizarre. The old family narrative of parents being mutually valued and devoted to caring for their children is overwritten with stories of abuse and alienation. Balanced reasoning in the search for commonality and compromise is replaced by extreme and unyielding accusations. Formerly respectful and well-behaved children become rude and callous toward one or both parents. Coparents' respect for one another's complicated humanity is replaced with overly simplistic, negative stereotypes.

Intractable parent-child contact problems can become living nightmares: tales of anger, resentment, and injustice; children caught in the middle; college funds drained by legal fees; children involved in police calls to the house; child protective services coming to the school to interview the children; children having stomach aches or headaches before parenting exchanges; or even a child self-harming in a parent's home or running away. Parent-child contact problems that become intractable and remain unresolved are malignant in the same way as high blood pressure is to heart disease.

In the next chapters, we examine how intractable parent-child contact problems build into a painful deadlock for the family, or what is known as a "hurting stalemate." We find that unless parents take time to understand how these problems develop, they won't be able to move away from family conflict and toward family peace.

CHAPTER 5: KEY POINTS

- Parent-child contact problems are intractable when they persist, and worsen in spite of multiple attempts to resolve them.
- The important point about intractable problems is that although they are difficult and may not yield to a total "cure," these problems are not hopeless. And, they can and need to be managed.

CHAPTER 6

Three Stages of Resist Refuse Problems

THREE STAGES OF RESIST REFUSE PROBLEMS

Sadly, intractable family conflicts are common in our history. In Shakespeare's play *Romeo and Juliet,* an intractable conflict between two families, the Montagues and the Capulets, led to the death of Romeo and Juliet. The most famous American family feud between the Hatfields and the McCoys began in 1882. Ironically, in 1979, members from both families appeared in the television program *Family Feud.* In 2000, the clans shared the first of what has become an annual joint family reunion, now called the Hatfield and McCoy Reunion Festival.[24] When clan descendants signed a truce in 2003, Reo Hatfield said, "We're not saying you don't have to fight, because sometimes you do have to fight. But you don't have to fight forever.[25]

The Hatfield Clan of the Hatfield-McCoy-feud. (Public domain)
Source: http://en.wikipedia.org/wiki/Image:HatfieldClan.jpg

Social scientists and almost everyone else have tried to understand intractable conflicts, whether they involve parent-child contact problems, family feuds, or international wars. The model we present is adapted from the work of international peace scholars.[26] According to the model, as the family conflict goes up, the family's functioning goes down. If an effective intervention is not made, eventually the parents find themselves in a "hurting stalemate," or a painful deadlock, in which they are unable to protect their children. At this juncture, it is up to the courts and behavioral health providers to guide the family past the grip of intractable family conflict, toward peace in family relationships.

Figure 5, the Family Conflict Curve, presents a roadmap for RRP, from problem onset to problem resolution. We find that sharing an overview of RRP illustrated by the Family Conflict Curve helps parents to better understand the nature of the problem they face, and the path to solution.

Figure 5: Family Conflict Curve

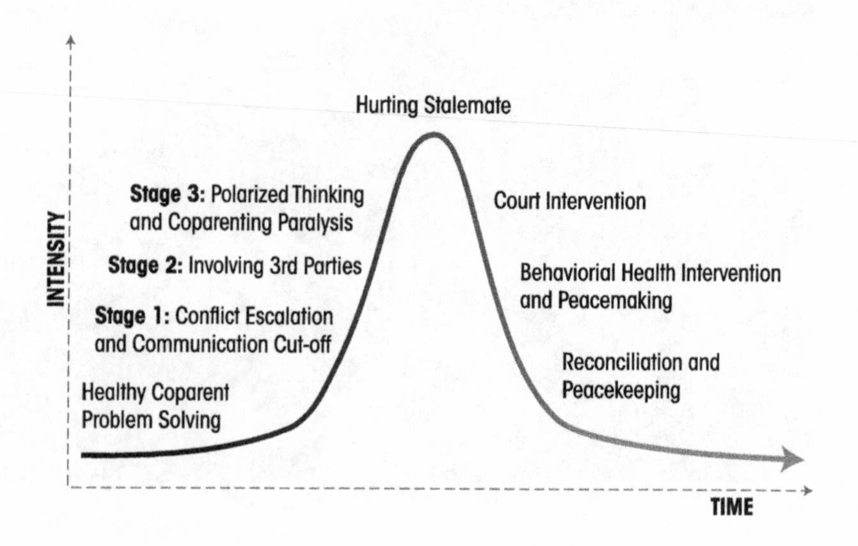

Healthy Coparent Problem-Solving

Even in normal families that successfully navigate the transitions of divorce, coparents may argue, bicker, blame, and misinterpret. They may also give each other the silent treatment. Their conflict may escalate into loud speech, lecturing rather than listening, threats, and insults. But the escalation is capped off by one means or another. The parents regroup. They return to the business of talking more reasonably about issues involving the children until they arrive at agreements about what to do. They resolve conflicts feeling more or less assured that a lesson has been learned, and the next time a similar problem arises, it will be handled better.

Minimal use of pressure is the hallmark of skillful coparenting. At this level, parents talk diplomatically and non-aggressively to each other about the problem using a "Can we talk?" approach. They know that whatever needs to be talked about is threatening and may get worse. To contain the threat, they avoid blaming one another for what went wrong. They keep the conversation child-focused and avoid personal commentary. They remain focused on the present, on neutral descriptions of what is going on, on possible solutions, and on developing a plan of action. They make "we" statements that affirm the importance of the coparenting relationship. Perhaps they share with each other the mutual difficulty of their circumstance. Or, they show that they understand their coparent's point of view by saying, "You've got a point." If the conversation veers toward defensiveness and verbal aggression, they manage to stay focused on the main issue rather than piggybacking issues on top of one another, or letting the discussion drift into theoretical speculations about the causes of the problem. They talk in soft, non-harsh tones. The conversation's pace is deliberate. They don't interrupt or talk over each other.

In healthy coparenting relationships when parent-child relationship challenges arise, the coparents stay present and future focused. They arrive at a shared understanding of what the facts are, what the facts mean, and how to problem-solve the situation. In families with RRP, coparents struggle to frame problems they face in shared terms. They have competing histories often full of partial truths about who did what to whom, how bad it was, for what reasons, what it means, and who is to blame. With such confusion, they are unable to agree on what to do. As an evaluator wrote in her report for family court, "Mother and Father have markedly different observations and beliefs about the children's emotional and behavioral problems. Not only do they disagree if the children have problems, they disagree on what the problems are, the root of their problems, the manifestations of their problems, and the solutions to their problems."

Stage 1: Conflict Escalation and Communication Cut-Off

These stages describe key patterns in the family that develop as RRP is made worse as conflict increases over time. In Stage 1, disagreements about what is best for the children escalate and do serious damage to the coparenting relationship. Coparents become skeptical and defensive; they become resistant to hearing one another's point of view. They lose faith that their coparent can be trusted and will act with good intentions. The coparent they once viewed as worthy of raising children with is now seen as a defective parent, not only wrong but somehow sick, and possibly unfit to be alone with the child.

As coparents become frustrated with their inability to communicate and problem-solve with one another, they resort to threats, allegations, and blame. For example, they may threaten to call the other parent's family or friends, their attorney, mental health professionals involved with the family, the police, or even child protective services. Sometimes they threaten retaliation with statements such as:

- "You'll never see the kids again."
- "I'll ruin you financially."
- I'll call your business partner to let them know what a liar and cheat you are."

- "I'll call the Internal Revenue Service and report how you have been cheating on your taxes."

Here are more examples of the kinds of threats coparents with escalated behavior make:

- One mom wrote, "And if Dad is spreading half-baked facts about a situation he knows nothing about, and causing more drama and anger for my sons and family, this is going to become a legal issue of slander."
- "I'm done fighting with you. I will listen to my children and what their needs are, not yours."
- "You ask me about the camp again one more time, just one more time, and find out how fast I have the police knocking on your door."
- "Are you really telling me that you are a responsible parent? Leave me alone. I'm going to call the police. And I'll be getting an order of protection against you. Contact me one more time, and I will get this done."
- "This is the last time I will opt for this. Let me see him this week or I will remove him from my insurance effective Friday. Your choice."
- "I have asked you two times to stay away from my sister. If you ever talk to her again it will be in direct defiance and disrespect to me, to her, and to my family. If you are going to insist on being a belligerent fool, and a coward, then I will treat you like one. Be prepared to deal with this in public."

Threatening behavior may even come from extended family members. At a child's sporting event, Paternal Grandmother said to the mom, "You're only here because Dad let you be here. You better watch out."

As threats escalate, coparents restrict their communication to emails and texts, and the tone of emails and texts becomes more formal and foreboding. For example, if a coparent begins an email or text with, "Yesterday I emailed you at 4:04 pm…" it sounds as if they want to create a document trail to nail the other parent about timeliness or some other type of accountability.

If escalated communication continues, one or both coparents will severely restrict communication. They may stop responding to emails or insist all communication go through their attorney. Restricting email and text communication may reduce coparenting conflict in the short run, but it increases the likelihood of problems for the children over the long run. When parents lack quick and easy access to accurate information about the well-being of the children, they usually fill in the blanks with fearful and anger-driven assumptions. As one parent said, "It's kinda a black box, my kid's life at his mom's." And in the absence of direct communication, coparents rely on the children's reports, which usually contain incomplete if not inaccurate information.

One parent said, "The kids would get in the car and complain to me about stuff. My parents were divorced so I know that conversation in the car, the petty complaints. I would say, 'This is gossipy. If you have issues about Mom, don't complain to me, talk to Mom.'" Pretty good response, right? Here are some examples of the unreliable information that children sometimes present parents:

- Two teenage girls begin refusing to see Dad in November. The coparents meet with an interventionist in February. Mom said Dad doesn't show the girls that he cares; he didn't even send holiday presents. Dad replied that when he was with the girls at Thanksgiving they told him what presents they wanted. He told them, "Ok, but I will have to get them during my next trip to China, so you won't have them in time for Christmas. They were okay with that."
- A father emails his therapist, "Michael texted me at 8:50 p.m. that his mother was squeezing his leg and that it really hurt. That was followed by a text from him at 9:01 p.m. saying never

mind, that he forgives her and they are friends. Both messages are disturbing. I'm increasingly more worried and upset. Michael is being hurt each week."

- During a custody evaluation, Mom reported that her daughter had told her that Dad was trying to poison her. Upon interview, the child explained that unlike Mom, Dad gave her milk and other foods whose expiration date had passed.

Effective communication between coparents is key to working on parent-child contact problems. If a resisted parent knows precious little about the child's day-to-day experiences as the parent tries to make their way back into the child's heart, they won't have many good ideas about topics for conversation or activities to offer the child. The resisted parent may also not have an accurate view of how the child experienced parenting time with them. They may think their parenting time went okay, but the child tells the favored parent that it was terrible. Children in families with RRP regularly provide different information to each parent. This happens when children are caught in between warring coparents. To cope with being caught in the war zone, a child will align with one side, avoid disappointing or angering a parent, or avoid having difficult conversations about tough relationship problems.

Stage 2: Involving Third Parties: Extended Family, Counselors, Police, the Courts

Coparents who are unable to talk through RRP usually turn to family members, friends, clergy and counselors for assistance. In healthier situations, extended family members of the favored parent may try to talk the child out of their resistance. They may remind the child of all they have to be grateful for, about the good times they enjoyed with the resisted parent in the past, or about the child's duty to forgive loved ones even when they have been hurtful. Sometimes they use guilt and shame to try to motivate the child. They may say, "You are really hurting Dad's feelings because he wants to see you." However, advice from family members to the child usually makes things worse. A good practice for both parents is to request that family and friends avoid talking about the divorce in front of or with the child.

For mild parent-child contact problems, professionals now generally agree that both parents can benefit from early education and possibly counseling to prevent escalation of the parent-child contact problem into an infinitely more problematic RRP. The extent of the professional intervention needed depends on the extent of RRP. As the RRP becomes more severe, both parents and the child will need to participate. However, the child does not typically want to work on their problems with the resisted parent, and they complain about having their schedule interrupted to go to counseling.

Later we discuss the types of ideas and skills development a counselor might offer for RRP, but at this point, we want to note that counseling is most effective when the resistance is addressed early, not when the conflict has escalated to malignant proportions. As with most health problems, early identification and intervention is key to successful outcomes. With cancer, diabetes, and many medical health conditions, it is well known that early intervention makes for easier and more successful treatment. Waiting may mean the condition gets so bad that it cannot be effectively treated.

When a child resists or refuses contact with a parent, often Mom and Dad are unable to agree on a plan to address the problem, including whether counseling is needed or who the counselor should be. If Mom and Dad are unable to agree, usually they turn to the court to break their deadlock.

Judges and attorneys appreciate that court is not a desirable approach for solving family problems. The courts encourage parents to reach agreements rather than fight it out. They may order mediation before the parents can present their case to the judge. The court may order the family to participate in a family intervention, even as they prepare for trial. If the family ends up in a court hearing, each parent will make a grueling series of complaints about their coparent that are certain to escalate coparenting and parent-child resistance.

Sometimes a parent's petitioning the court to decide custody and parenting-time disputes puts the family into Stage 2 conflict, but in families with intractable conflict, often there has already been involvement of the police or child protective services. There are times that calling the police is the only safe choice. Domestic violence, child abuse, child neglect, substance abuse, and mental illness are very real problems that can endanger the child. If a parent refuses to comply with the court-ordered parenting time schedule, asking the police to enforce the current prevailing court order may be reasonable. If a parent is fearful that conflict may get out of hand when they go to the marital home to remove their personal property, asking for a police standby may be necessary.

But involving the police or child protective services is "going nuclear" in terms of conflict escalation unless the circumstances truly require such action. A parent's humiliation, fear, and anger that accompany being arrested or unjustly investigated for child abuse can result in an "unforgivable injury." Similarly, the coparenting relationship might never recover if a parent is arrested in front of the child.

Parents who involve police or child protective services can be naive about their coparent's retaliation following a call to the police. Parents who involve legal authorities tend to think they are doing what any caring and reasonable parent would do, or they are angry and alarmed to the point they don't much care about the consequences of involving the legal authorities. However, they may later agree that getting their families out of involvement with the legal and court system is critical. Again, there are lots of times that involving police and child protective services is the only reasonable choice. But police and child protective services often conclude there was no child abuse or maltreatment. It's like a coach at a football game who calls for a review of a referee's call on the field. If the review shows the referee's call was correct, the coach gets punished by losing a timeout. When a parent's allegation to police or child protective services is unfounded or unsubstantiated, the accused parent will probably feel justified in retaliating against their coparent in one way or another.

Here are some examples of parents allowing conflict to escalate that result in calls to the authorities that could have been avoided:

- Mom moves out. She comes back to the marital residence to retrieve personal property. When she arrives, she finds that Father's older daughter from a previous marriage is watching the kids. Mom calls the police to have the older daughter removed from the house.
- A father's four-year-old daughter develops a urinary tract infection. Dad takes her to the pediatrician who prescribes an antibiotic cream. Dad has his new girlfriend show his daughter how to apply the cream. When Mother learns the new girlfriend had looked at the child's private parts and watched her apply the lotion, Mother calls Child Protective Services. She also refuses Father's next scheduled parenting time. He then calls the police.
- A mother and child were invited to a birthday party of the child's friend. The mother attended though it was Father's parenting day. When the father learned the mother was at the party, he had paternal grandparents go to the party to retrieve the child. The mother and paternal grandparents argued. The police were called.

Stage 3: Polarized Thinking and Coparenting Paralysis

As family conflict escalates, the number of contested issues increases, and conflict emerging from any of these contested issues can trigger an outburst. Parents find themselves spiraling downward into an emotional whirlpool in which avoiding conflict becomes increasingly difficult. Prolonged exposure to escalated conflict stress-loads the family and sets up further conflict. Coparents continue to have conflict because they have already had so much conflict. Conflict escalation becomes a toxic force in the family that is more difficult to organize and manage than any maladaptive personality trait the individual parents may have.

Repeated experiences of escalated RRP conflict result in strikingly similar patterns across a wide variety of family types. The kinds of similarities we observe across families is illustrated by a judge who stated these observations about a family:

- The parties have a hostile and adversarial relationship.
- Both parties are actively "looking for" problems regarding the children's care by the other party.
- Both parties are hoping to find problems with the other parent, and are willing to believe allegations regarding the other parent's deficiencies.
- Neither party is entirely truthful or credible.
- Both parties have lingering and unresolved anger issues regarding their marriage and dissolution.
- Both parties have allowed their hostility with the other party to cloud their judgment.
- The parties are apparently unable to see their own conflict, the deficiencies that it creates in their parenting skills, and the effect that it has had and is likely to have in the future on the children.
- Neither party is likely to agree with the court's assessment in this ruling, and both are likely to continue to assign sole responsibility for their issues to the other parent.

CHAPTER 6: KEY POINTS

- In families with RRP, coparents have competing stories about who did what to whom, how bad it was, for what reasons, what it means, and who is to blame. With such confusion, they are unable to agree on what to do.
- The coparent they once viewed as worthy of raising children with is now seen as a defective parent, not only wrong but somehow sick, and possibly unfit to be alone with the child.
- When parents lack quick and easy access to accurate information about the well-being of the children, they usually fill in the blanks with fearful and anger-driven assumptions.
- As with most health problems, early identification and intervention for RRP is key to successful outcomes.
- When a parent's allegation to police or child protective services is unfounded or unsubstantiated, the accused parent will probably feel justified in retaliating against their coparent in one way or another.
- Coparents continue to have conflict because they have already had so much conflict. Conflict escalation becomes a toxic force in the family that is more difficult to organize and manage than any maladaptive personality trait the individual parents may have.

CHAPTER 7

The Three Dementors of Resist Refuse Problems

THE THREE DEMENTORS OF RESIST REFUSE PROBLEMS

"Dementors" are imagined creatures created by J.K. Rowling, the author of the Harry Potter book series.[27] Dementors are dark creatures that consume human happiness, creating an ambiance of coldness, darkness, misery, and despair. Because of their power to drain happiness and hope from humans, they have been given the duty of being guards at Azkaban, the prison for wizards, where they prevent the prisoners from having the will or ability to escape.

We use the term "Dementors" to describe the negative effects of high-conflict divorce on the way family members think, respond emotionally, and engage one another. Repeated exposure to escalated RRP conflict "dements" the mind with harmful thinking and emotional patterns that often leads to misery and despair. Usually family members do not notice when they are showing a Dementor's negative influence, though they may recognize it in the behavior of their coparent or child. For example, resisted parents usually say their child's thinking and emotions toward them are distorted and perplexing. The power of the Dementors is so great that if a therapist points out to a parent that they are under the influence of a Dementor, perhaps by expressing an overly negative stereotyping of their coparent, the parent may accuse the therapist of failing to understand what they have been through, or accuse them of being biased and aligned with the coparent.

Dementor 1: Inability to Address Truth and Blame

> "There ain't no answer. There ain't gonna be any answer.
> There never has been an answer. That is the answer."
>
> **–Gertrude Stein**

For a lot of reasons, parents feel it is critical to establish the "truth" about what happened and who is responsible for what happened that led to RRP. It is common for parents to think, "How are we going to solve the problem if we don't know the truth about what the problem is and who caused it? Good question, but the family will not be able to agree on an answer. Regardless of whether one or both parents were the cause of RRP, the critical issue is restoring the child's relationship with the resisted parent.

Coparents always have contradictory explanations for what happened—the resisted parent says the child's affections have been alienated by the favored parent; the favored parent says the child's resistance is justified and in response to the rejected parent's poor parenting. Each parent's explanation, which is usually partially valid, is held as a complete and accurate description of the cause of the problem. Typically their position is that the problem is being caused exclusively by the other parent.

As we described in Chapter 4, many combinations of reasons can result in a child resisting contact with a parent, so it is important to avoid labeling the situation as coming from a single cause. But a characteristic of intractable conflict is that the more threatening and complex the issues are, the more the parents are driven toward overly simplified ideas about the nature and source of the problems. As a colleague observed, "We end up with deceptively easy answers from people who are desperate."

The best course is for coparents to suspend talking about the past. For example, it is natural to reach into an ongoing problem's past, but the briefest mention of a past problem can be like tipping the first domino in a long row—the conversation quickly escalates into blame and counter-blame, and the coparents' ability to problem-solve spins out of control. We advise parents, "Problems that need to be talked about can be talked about as they currently exist."

The same prohibition about discussing the past does not hold true for the relationship between the child and the resisted parent. The child's resistance is squarely constructed on their grievances about the resisted parent. Restoration of good will between the parent and the child depends on effectively addressing the child's grievances, even if the child's allegations are not based in reality and are instead, distorted. We delve into this issue later when we examine the resentment that RRP invariably generates in family members.

Dementor 2: Polarized Thinking

Intractable RRP changes the psychology of family members in undesirable ways. Parents and children develop polarized thinking that divides the coparenting relationship and other family members into opposing camps. For example, Dad and two teenage sons were devastated when Mom had an affair and immediately moved out and into the home of her new significant other. Dad and the two boys responded by each getting the same tattoo that read, "Family forever." Dad did not seem to realize that the tattoos defined him and the two sons as being in one camp, and Mom in another.

Polarized thinking is not impartial. It involves different kinds of thinking errors. Three that we commonly find in families with parent-child contact problems are:

- Using stereotypes
- Drawing open-and-shut conclusions
- Ignoring negative confirmation bias

Stereotyped thinking lacks individuality. Coparents characterize one another with all negative attributes, rather than as human beings with a mixture of strengths and weaknesses. Ask the coparents to describe one another's parenting strengths and weaknesses. The list of weaknesses is long and detailed. The list of strengths tends to be something such as, "He's a good provider," or "She cares about the kids," or, "I don't know, I haven't seen him parent for a long time." Sometimes the identified strength is said sarcastically, for example, "He buys them a lot of things."

Here are some examples of stereotypes that family members offered of one another:

- "He was an absent husband and an absent father."
- A dad says about a mom who is having discipline problems with their 8-year-old son, "Mom wants to have 'robot' children. She does not want them to act out at all."
- "If I had not filed for child support, he would have disappeared and not come back. He thinks of her [their child] as a tool, not a human being with feelings."
- "It seems that Dad is disconnected from any real natural feelings. He is stiff, like he does not have the natural nurturing instinct."

Polarized stereotyped thinking often involves seeing one's coparent as having malicious motivations:

- "I think she's motivated by money, not a desire to have a child in her life."
- "I don't have an agenda, other than to ensure that she grows up and is happy. Her father has a different agenda, to have power struggles with me. His decision-making is not motivated by what is best for her."
- "Mom is forcing him to play left-handed baseball when he is clearly right-handed. She is left-handed and does not want him to be anything like me."
- "You're showing that you view the children as objects to be won, and you use their feelings to get, gain, or inflict punishments on me. This is your core. It doesn't matter if you deny it. Your actions are what they are. They are the fruit of your tree."
- "I don't feel that he really has her best interests in mind. It is more about his image and ego than anything."
- "I strongly believe that because of his childhood, he does not know love, only sex; that is love to him."
- "You have shown me what your idea of love is and it's corrupted, damaging, and emotionally abusive."

Polarized thinking leads to *open-and-shut conclusions*, that is, judgments presented as obvious, clear-cut, perfectly simple, and unambiguous truths. As the journalist H. L. Mencken said, "For every complex problem there is an answer that is clear, simple, and wrong."

Here are examples of children's *open-and-shut conclusions* about the resisted parent:

- "Every time we are sick or injured, he never believes us."
- "He said to me once that the only reason he wants us in his life is that he would not have to pay full child support."
- "He blames Mom for everything. He has told us multiple times that she is the main reason we are in therapy. He doesn't accept responsibility for anything."
- "She's hated me since I was little."
- "Every time I come home from being with him I feel that I disappointed my mom and sister. He has been such a bad person to both of them. He abused Mom when they were married, and he keeps that up now."
- "It would not change my opinion if you got help; there is no amount of help you could get to change you. If you cared you would not do any of this. You would have repented and not have forced me to go through all this."

Here are some examples of coparents' *open-and-shut conclusions*:

- "Something is going on while she is in Father's care; I believe that 100 percent. I don't know what, or who is doing it, but something bad is happening."
- "I am now very seriously concerned about what is going on in your household, in terms of how the children are being cared for and protected. Children always tell the truth."
- "Your recklessness with my kids is disgusting. Your intimidation with my kids is sickening. You are a failure as a father."

- "With one swipe of the pen, the judge stole my fatherhood."
- "I don't care what you think or about you at all."

Negative confirmation bias is the tendency to search for, interpret, focus on, and remember information in a way that confirms one's beliefs. Negative confirmation bias is one of the principal reasons that parent-child contact problems are intractable. Evidence showing the resisted parent has developed better parenting skills is ignored. Evidence indicating the favored parent is not alienating the children is ignored. In families with severe RRP, we sometimes make the point to the resisted parent about the strength of negative confirmation bias by quoting the Miranda warning that police recite when making an arrest, "Everything you say can and will be used against you."

Peter Coleman, PhD, an intractable conflict scholar, wrote, "For a person in the throes of a powerful, long-term conflict, misperception and misunderstanding rule. Concerns over obtaining accurate information [are replaced by] defending our sense of the Truth and what is Right. These may of course be valid concerns. But when everything makes perfect sense in a complicated conflict, when who the good guys and the bad guys are is perfectly clear, we must be all the more vigilant [about the tendency toward biased thinking]."[28]

Robin Vallacher, PhD, another intractable conflict scholar, identified two patterns of negative confirmation bias that are relevant to parents: 1) they tend to deny or discount any and all positive information about their coparent; and 2) they feel *overwhelming resistance* (emphasis added) to acting differently toward the person they view as causing misery to them and their children.[29]

Here is an example of negative confirmation bias from a child:

Question: Can you think of anything good about your dad?"

Answer: I cannot. You know something is wrong when you have to try to conjure up good thoughts about someone. I'm most concerned that he will sit here [in the interventionist's office] and act and pretend that he cares. He cries, but it is fake crying. The only time I saw him crying was at his mother's funeral, but there were no tears or Kleenex, so I don't think he was crying; he was putting on an act."

In short, the devastating stress of parent-child contact problems results in polarized thinking that leads family members to draw conclusions about one another that are polarized (lacking cooperation), stereotyped (lacking individuality), and open-and-shut (lacking flexibility). Negative confirmation bias restricts the impact of healing information and experience. Although a resisted parent may work earnestly for a long time to engage the child in fun and loving ways, the parent may see only small, occasional signs that the child's resistance toward them is softening. Occasionally, the parents and children are simultaneously ready to close the book on conflict and open a new chapter of family relationships, but usually the process is *sloooow*. And during the reunification process between a parent and a child when family members are on red alert, a parent's small slipup can trigger a family member's underlying negative mindsets and resentments, leading to despair that change is even possible.

Dementor 3: Deep Resentment

When coparents are working toward de-escalated conflict, distinguishing between facts and feelings is critical. Facts are external, observable events subject to public confirmation, for example, whether or not the temperature went below freezing last night. Feelings are internal, private, and subjective rather than objective. If one imagines a landscape that includes a river, the land represents facts; the river represents feelings. The river carves the shape of the land. Resentment is a feeling that arises in response to facts and the interpretation of those facts. Resentment carves a deep canyon between the two sides in a parent-child contact problem.

To resolve parent-child contact problems, working on the feelings that emerge from the facts is critical. Arguing about whether it is more accurate to define the problem as alienation rather than justified rejection accomplishes little. At the feelings level, the family is coping with a lot of different emotions: hurt, anger, hatred, unjustness, unfairness, frustration, outrage. Family members feel insulted, belittled, embittered, incensed, antagonized, infuriated, disgruntled, irritated, over-stressed, and more. These kinds of feelings lead to resentment and must be dealt with if the parent-child relationship is to be healed.

The Merriam-Webster Dictionary defines *resentment* as, "A feeling of indignant displeasure or persistent ill will at something regarded as a wrong, insult, or injury." Resentment often involves a sense of being victimized by an injustice. Resentment is especially powerful when it is felt toward a family member; it leaves one feeling betrayed. Resentment results in a powerful urge to withdraw from the person and cut off communication.

Here are some statements made by children that reflect resentment:

- A teen said, "I think I would hurt her if I saw her. I told my family I cannot see my mother again; I would hurt her, but only her. I don't get angry; that's not for me. She has caused so much pain to everybody. It's not fair that she does not suffer as much as we do."
- "To be honest, I hate him. He's mean. I don't think he cares. I don't think it is getting better and he's going to therapy. I hate the way he treats other people. I hate his mentality that he is right with everything. Nobody else can have a valid point. I am so sick of it. I want him away from me for a long time so that I can remember why I like him."

Here are some statements by coparents that reflect resentment:

- A father alleged through his attorney, "Mother also makes a false claim and slanderous attack against Father by stating 'Father seeks parenting time with the minor child (likely for financial reasons).' This paragraph is beyond repulsive, is full of lies, and is offensive, disrespectful, and demeaning to Child's Father, and to all the effort he has put forth and the financial burden he's had to carry just to have some peace and the ability to care for his child."

- A father wrote, "It is impossible to put into words how much Father has been abused and harassed by Mother, and what he's had to do, endure, and to put up with in order to be an involved father in Child's life; he has done so at great expense, both emotionally and financially. Stepmother has experienced nearly all the strife Father has as well."
- A mom said, "I felt so betrayed. I came home and everything was gone, the furniture, the kids, and their clothing, the legal papers, the family pictures. Then I find out he had a private investigator following me."
- "Asking to move 2,000 miles away with my child is like stabbing me in the heart."

Resentment is a lasting feeling of ill will caused by an act regarded as unfair, wrong, insulting, or hurtful. Resentment can result in a grudge, an unforgiving mindset, an unwillingness to admit one's own mistakes, and a wish for revenge—or at least a lack of compassion for the suffering of family members.[30] Working on resentments and grudges is the deep work of conflict de-escalation.

The Predictable Irrationality of RRP

Our observation is that families subjected to the extended distress of RRP become "predictably irrational"; that is, their capacity for critical thinking, communicating about RRP, and interacting with the resisted parent is compromised. For example, coparents invariably view the other as "out of touch with reality" in one way or another. A resisting child usually overestimates the likelihood of being unsafe with the resisted parent and underestimates the likelihood of ever again having a good relationship with the resisted parent.

It is curious that *almost always* family members are plagued by the irrationality of the Dementors. What accounts for this? The reason family members are almost always impacted by the Dementors is because of the way RRP stress impacts their nervous systems. To understand how this happens, you have to know a little bit about the body's autonomic nervous system (ANS). The ANS has two main branches: 1)the sympathetic nervous system (which activates the body), and 2) the parasympathetic nervous system (which relaxes the body).

When confronted with danger, the sympathetic nervous system activates into fight-flight-freeze. Rebecca Bailey, PhD, using Polyvagal Theory, explains that the parasympathetic nervous system has two sub-branches: One branch, in response to threat, activates social engagement and connection. The other activates collapse and disconnection when the level of danger is overwhelming.[31]

The two branches of the ANS act together when the body senses danger. With low levels of threat, the parasympathetic nervous system automatically encourages social engagement and connection. When the threat level is moderate, the sympathetic nervous system automatically activates into fight-flight-freeze. When the threat level is severe, the parasympathetic nervous system can produce collapse and disconnection. In both the fight-flight-freeze mode and a state of collapse and disconnection, a parent's or child's capacity for critical thinking, communicating about RRP, and interacting with the polarized parent is compromised.

Within this framework, the presence of the Dementors in the family reflects an *adaptive* response to extraordinary stress. The challenge for parents and behavioral health professionals responding to the alienation crisis is to create safe spaces for the family. It is only when family members feel reasonably safe that they can overcome the negative pull toward collapse and disconnection, and stay centered in their best thinking.

CHAPTER 7: KEY POINTS

- We use the term "Dementors" to describe the negative effects of high-conflict divorce on the way family members think, respond emotionally, and engage one another. Repeated exposure to escalated RRP conflict "dements" the mind with harmful thinking and emotional patterns that often lead to misery and despair.

- The devastating stress of parent-child contact problems results in family members drawing conclusions about one another that are polarized (lacking cooperation), stereotyped (lacking individuality), and open-and-shut (lacking flexibility). Negative confirmation bias restricts the impact of healing information and experience.

- Working on resentments and grudges is the deep work of conflict de-escalation.

- A characteristic of intractable conflict is that the more threatening and complex the issues are, the more the parents are driven toward overly simplified ideas about the nature and source of the problems.

CHAPTER 8

Moving from Coparenting Paralysis to Coordination: Hurting Stalemates and Court Interventions

MOVING FROM COPARENTING PARALYSIS TO COORDINATION: HURTING STALEMATES AND COURT INTERVENTIONS

Eventually, the toll of the conflict on the family becomes unbearable. The parents become battle weary. The emotional and financial resources of the family have been depleted. The misery of the children is obvious. The coparents enter what is referred to as a *Hurting Stalemate.*[32]

A hurting stalemate occurs after conflict develops to the point that neither side seems able to win, but neither side wants to back down. Despite realizing that the conflict is going nowhere, it is difficult for parents who have polarized thoughts and attitudes about each other to consider a settlement. They are fearful of the other side and do not want to go through the difficult conversations needed to resolve their differences.

Stalemates emerge for several reasons. Resources to continue the conflict may have been depleted, or the cost of the conflict may have become too great. In the families we work with, it is common to hear one or both parents say something like, "I just want this to be over. It is a nightmare. The kids' college funds have been spent, I have maxed-out my credit cards, and now my parents are dipping into their savings to pay court costs. I am sick of it; my friends are sick of hearing about it. I offered to sit down with him/her and work this out between just the two of us, but all I got back was a nasty letter from his/her attorney."

A famous speech by Chief Joseph of the Nez Perce Indian Nation expresses the hurting stalemate of his people:

> "Tell General Howard I know his heart. What he told me before, I have it in my heart. I am tired of fighting. Our Chiefs are killed; Looking Glass is dead, Ta Hool Hool Shute is dead. The old men are all dead. It is the young men who say yes or no. He who led on the young men is dead. It is cold, and we have no blankets; the little children are freezing to death. My people, some of them, have run

> away to the hills, and have no blankets, no food. No one knows where they are — perhaps freezing to death. I want to have time to look for my children, and see how many of them I can find. Maybe I shall find them among the dead. Hear me, my Chiefs! I am tired; my heart is sick and sad. From where the sun now stands I will fight no more forever."

When RRP exists, moving from stalemate into conflict de-escalation can be hard. Both parents need to be ready to come to the negotiating table. Usually the resisted parent is in a hurry to restore the parent-child relationship, while the favored parent doubts that reunification will be possible anytime soon. If the child has been allowed to cut off contact with the resisted parent, the child is often less stressed and better adjusted at home and in school. The child's improvement is taken as proof-positive that the resisted parent's involvement was toxic for the child. The favored parent hesitates to encourage reunification, fearing that reunification will compromise the child's gains. The child may think it is no big deal that they do not have an active relationship with the resisted parent, and the favored parent finds it hard if not impossible to motivate the child to address the relationship problem.

Families can remain in the hurting stalemate because they are unclear about what they could try in order to address it. A father wrote to his son:

> "It is with a heavy heart that I write you this letter. It has now been over one-half year since we last spoke. I know that very harsh words were exchanged between us, painful words. I hope that we can someday talk about this and try to resolve this issue, and I think there will be a time for this in the future [...] You may ask yourself why? Why after all this time is he reaching out to me? Well, the reason is that after our fight, I felt really hurt and demoralized. I felt that I had not only lost my family, but that I was also losing my children. First my marriage, then your older brother,

> and now you. I guess I just gave up. I thought in time you would figure things out and come around. I guess I had no answers to what was happening and didn't really know how to fix things. To be honest with you, I don't know how to fix things now. But I do know that inaction is not the right path and I also know how I feel."

Parents may not be motivated to engage more cooperatively because one or both want an evaluation to prove their coparent has a mental condition or a parenting skills deficiency that should merit a reduction in their parenting time. The resisted parent may want reunification, but also want to have their day in court to prove that they are the victims of alienation. The favored parent may want the court to certify that the resisted parent is an abuser who deserves the rejection he is getting from the child. Or, a parent may be reluctant to settle on a parenting plan because they want to fight for an award of attorney fees. Their position is, "What you did is so wrong that I should get reimbursed for having to defend myself against you."

In short, parents can be suffering the pain of intractable RRP, but conclude that they need the court to hear the case and rule on critical issues before they will be motivated to negotiate solutions to RRP.

Sometimes the court's orders do not move the parents past their hurting stalemate. For example, if a parent thinks the judge missed the call—failing to recognize how abusive Dad has been or how alienating Mom is—then this parent may believe that the court-ordered parenting plan does not adequately protect the children. The dissatisfied parent may appeal the court's ruling, a legal maneuver that restarts the litigation escalation. Or, the dissatisfied parent may undermine the implementation of the court-ordered plan. They express their dissatisfaction by complying with the "letter" of the court-ordered plan, but not its "spirit." They may send the children to the resisted parent's home. But when told the kids are being rude and disrespectful, the dissatisfied parent does little or nothing to get them to behave respectfully toward the resisted parent, as they would expect in any other circumstance.

When the court-ordered parenting plan is not accepted by both parents, the conflict remains intractable. The court's intervention becomes another failed attempt to resolve it, and the parents may find themselves back in their attorneys' offices climbing to new heights of conflict and new depths of misery. However, we find that the ongoing suffering of RRP almost always motivates the parents to search for solutions to their hurting stalemate. Then the stage is set for coordinated conflict reduction and peacemaking.

Family Conflict Curve

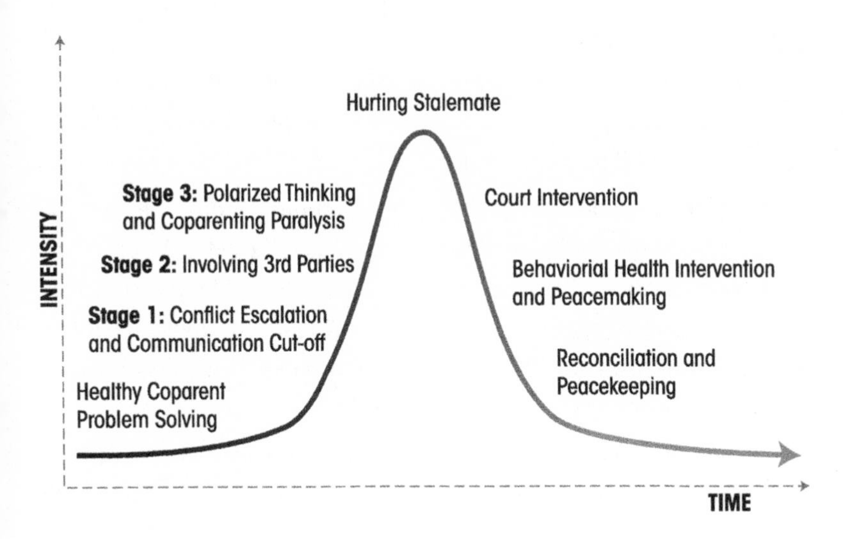

Court Interventions to De-escalate Conflict

When parents are unable to negotiate an agreement about how to approach RRP, they need a detailed court-ordered parenting plan to guide the family. The plan typically spells out who will have legal decision-making authority (also known as "legal custody") regarding the child's medical care, education, activities, and religious training. The plan establishes the regular and holiday parenting time schedules, with specific start and ending times for each parent. The rule of thumb is that the more conflict the parents have and the less ability they have to meet and negotiate problems, the more detailed the parenting plan needs to be. For example, a detailed parenting plan may order where parenting time exchanges are to occur, who is responsible for transporting the child, what options should be used if a parent is unavailable to provide childcare during their parenting time, what happens if an emergency medical decision needs to be made about the child, and how and when the child has communication with the non-custodial parent.

Typically, the court orders families with RRP into treatment. In this book, we refer to such treatment as "RRP family therapy." Behavioral health professionals use various approaches to treat RRP. The provider must have the right skills set; that is, they must have training and experience in working with families with RRP. And it is important that the provider is "forensically informed"; that is, the provider has received training in how to deliver behavioral health services when a family is involved in family court.

In general, more severe problems require more intervention resources, and the earlier the intervention is made, the better the prognosis for a good outcome. The type of interventions ordered by the court can vary significantly. We strongly believe that a *family systems approach* is necessary to resolve RRP. This approach seeks to understand how family members' interactions play into RRP.

Further, it looks at how RRP is influenced by people outside the immediate family, including the courts and behavioral health professionals. The problem developed as a product of a complex system of interactions among all immediate family relationships and others involved with the family. An effective solution to the problem will require changes in all of the family members and in their relationship patterns. It is an oversimplification to think that the problem exists only between the child and the resisted parent, or within the resisted parent or favored parent. Approaching the problem with this view is a setup for failure.

CHAPTER 8: KEY POINTS

- Usually the resisted parent is in a hurry to restore the parent-child relationship, while the favored parent doubts that reunification will be possible anytime soon.
- Parents suffering the pain of intractable RRP often are not motivated to negotiate solutions to RRP. They conclude that the court needs to hear their case and rule on critical issues before they are willing to negotiate solutions to RRP.
- When parents are unable to negotiate an agreement about how to approach RRP, they need a detailed court-ordered parenting plan to guide the family.
- Typically, the court orders families with RRP into treatment.
- We strongly believe that a family systems approach is necessary to resolve RRP. This approach seeks to understand how family members' interactions play into RRP.
- An effective solution to RRP requires change in all of the family members and in their relationship patterns.

PART TWO:
33 SOLUTIONS FOR FREQUENTLY ENCOUNTERED COPARENTING PROBLEMS

"No family is perfect. The best we can hope for is a family that is functional most of the time, makes allowances for some dysfunction, and when things break down, finds a way to mend them."

–David Richo

INDEX TO 33 COPARENTING SOLUTIONS

Chapter 9

Chapter 10
Coparenting Solutions: Responding to Your Child's Complaints

Chapter 11
Coparenting Solutions: Responding to Your Child's Resistance

CHAPTER 9

Coparenting Solutions for Improving Communication

COPARENTING SOLUTIONS FOR IMPROVING COMMUNICATION

The topic of parenting is widely written about.[33] Many of the 33 coparenting solutions we present apply to divorce and separation situations that do not include RRP but are characterized by intractable coparenting conflict that may lead to RRP.

Even in well-adjusted and intact families, parents struggle with differences in parenting style. Sometimes parenting style differences are the single most important factor leading to separation and divorce. When an intractable RRP develops in the family, it is inevitable that coparenting will be horribly difficult. Those same parenting style differences that made life difficult when parents were together may now be viewed as signs of character deficits in the other parent. Sharing child-focused information becomes inefficient and riddled with stinging commentary. Coparents are presented with supersized challenges. Their emotional reserves are tested and exhausted repeatedly.

It has been said that the opposite of love is not hate, but indifference. Indifference allows for disengagement. A parent who disengages when conflict begins to boil can maintain emotional neutrality toward their coparent. Emotional neutrality allows them to keep their best thinking and coping skills intact. Remember, conflict escalation is the problem, not conflict. Conflict is inevitable in all relationships. Skillful management of conflict is what you and your child needs. We refer to parents who disengage from the whirlwind of conflict escalations as "Neutral Coparents."

"Escalated Coparents" get caught up in conflict escalation. They get fixated on the other parent's behavior as the sole cause of the problem. They are unable to stay focused on their own wisdom, and the escalation of coparenting conflict changes their bodies and minds. Their minds are hijacked by anger, and their bodies are flooded with fear and anger-related chemicals that make them vulnerable to compromised judgments and reactive behaviors.

Each parent can be both Escalated and Neutral at different points in time. We are trying to help you be more often a Neutral Parent in your approach to your coparent. Here is a summary of characteristics we find are associated with Escalated Coparents and Neutral Coparents.

Escalated Coparent	Neutral Coparent
Being right is top priority	Emotional regulation is top priority
Uncontained stress	Self-soothing, detachment
Accuses, blames, threatens	Takes responsibility for their behavior
Withdraws from communication	Seeks clarification of issues
Polarized thinking	Uses relative terms such as "likely" and "may"
Overconfidence in own ideas	Assumes there is more to be known

We have found that some coparenting problems and situations are shared among the families with RRP. In the Coparenting Solutions sections of the book, we present 33 commonly encountered coparenting challenges, and offer suggestions for how an "Escalated Coparent" versus a "Neutral Coparent" might respond.

1 What are some guidelines for how coparents can best use email and text messaging?

The following email guidelines are suggested:

- Use a business relationship model. The business is related to the welfare of your child. The business that needs to be transacted is information sharing, coordination of schedules and activities, and requests for changes. The tone is formal, polite, and respectful, without personal commentary. Begin with a polite greeting such as "Hi John" and end with a respectful "Sincerely" or "Best Regards."
- Limit the number of messages. Parents should not send more than two new emails per day, each with one topic per email, unless an emergency exists. No emails should be sent on the weekend unless urgent.
- Respond to emails within 48 hours for routine matters, and as soon as possible for emails marked "Urgent" in the subject line. If the receiver needs more time to respond, they should indicate this need, together with a specific time frame for responding.
- The email should be one short paragraph, no more than five sentences in length.
- The communication should be either: 1) future-focused regarding an emerging problem, or 2) informative, such as providing information from a medical appointment.
- The content of the email must pertain to the child rather than money, property, etc.
- If the email involves something transactional (a requested change in the schedule, etc.), the requesting parent should include a specific proposal to address the issue.
- If a parent wishes to make a proposal, include WHO does WHAT, WHEN, and WHERE. The response to a proposal should be a clear "Yes," "No," or a counterproposal.

- Each item should be said only once (no repeating what was said in the past).
- Keep communication factual and neutral. Avoid emotion and judgment. No abusive, insulting, sarcastic, or profane language. NO CAPITAL LETTERS FOR EMPHASIS!!!
- Emails should be between parents rather than a stepparent to a parent, unless otherwise agreed.
- If you and your coparent cannot refrain from violating these rules, consider using a coparenting app that includes communication documentation and/or editing such as ProperComm, coParenter, or OurFamilyWizard.

2 What if my coparent does not respond to emails or texts?

If your coparent does not respond to an email or text that you sent, you may feel ignored, dismissed, devalued, or brushed off. Your first impulse may be to send an escalated email such as, "This is the third time I've asked you if I can have extra time with the kids when my family is in town!" Or, you may send more emails or texts repeating your original message. The neutral response would be using your best diplomatic skills to send a follow-up communication requesting a specific time frame for a reply. For example, "I hope you got my earlier email about my family's upcoming visit. I sent it three days ago. I hope everything is okay on your end. I'd like to make plans for their visit and would appreciate hearing from you at your earliest convenience about what options might exist for extra time with the kids on that weekend." If you do not receive a response after your follow-up email and you need to decide or take an action, send your coparent an email stating your intent to decide on a plan within a certain amount of time. For example, "I continue to work on plans for my family's visit. We have yet to clarify what the schedule for the kids will be, but I need to purchase tickets for the baseball game. My plan is to purchase six tickets for the game this coming Wednesday, assuming that you will arrange for the kids to go to the game with us. Thanks for helping me in my planning. Regards, Phillip."

3 What if my coparent makes rude, sarcastic, or demeaning statements in an email or text?

Your coparent writes, "I got another report from the teacher that the kids not completing their homework is a problem. Seems to be another example of your problem with getting organized and following through." After reading a message like this, you will likely feel hurt, angry, and tempted to respond in kind. The Escalated Coparent says what the composed, Neutral Coparent only thinks. The Escalated Coparent writes something like, "You are such a control freak." The Neutral Coparent ignores the fight. They engage in self-talk that sounds something like, "My relationship with this person is over. I want to care less and less about their anger and aggression. I won't let them hook me back into their misery by provoking me. I will stay focused on the business of parenting, focus on the signal and ignore the noise." Then the Neutral Coparent writes, "I totally agree that the kids completing their homework is a top priority. I'll look into the teacher's report." Over time it will become more and more obvious who is fanning the flames of the conflict. Ignoring the provocation often results in a decrease in negative commentary coming from the coparent.

4 What if my coparent writes really long emails that include lots of inaccurate statements?

Unless you are a famous person who is used to being misunderstood and feeling unappreciated, inaccurate statements are tough to ignore. Many parents worry that if they do not set the record straight, it can be used against them later in court. The escalated response would be to write back an equally long, or longer, email or text to correct the record. This may seem to be the only way to protect yourself against future litigation. However, it is unlikely that your response would be the last word on the issues. A battle of words likely would continue and distract you from *what really matters—quality parenting.*

A Neutral Coparent would write something like, "I don't agree with much of what you wrote, but I am not going to address those disagreements now, especially in an email. A couple of points you made are directly relevant to coparenting the kids, so I'll respond to those...." It is wise to begin addressing the issues by identifying points the coparent made that you agree with; for example, "I agree that the kids feel anxious when it is time for them to go from one home to the other." You may want to point out specific issues you dispute; for example, "I especially do not agree with your statement that the kids are not safe in my care." To close the dialogue, you could state that you don't plan to talk anymore about this issue at this time as it will not be constructive.

What if emails appear to be coming from my coparent's spouse or partner under the coparent's name or email address?

Even if a coparent has a good relationship with a stepparent, receiving emails from the stepparent under the coparent's name is an invitation for confusion. If a coparent does not have a good relationship with a stepparent and is receiving emails from them, the coparent may feel manipulated, doubly misunderstood, and mistreated. The coparent could call them out and respond, "You've never spoken or written like that before, and I don't believe you wrote it. Tell X to mind their own business." However, this is likely to escalate conflict with the coparent and damage the relationship with the stepparent. Instead, a Neutral Coparent could choose a response such as this: "I am confused. Your email appears to have come from your account, but seems to have been written by your partner/spouse. That makes me uncomfortable. I prefer that you and I communicate about the kids. Can we agree that any communication about the kids will be only between you and me?"

If the coparent does not accept the conciliatory request, the Neutral Coparent could follow up by writing something like, "I'm disappointed that we can't reach an agreement that only you and I will email about the kids. Emails from X are unwelcomed, and I will not respond to them." However, if the email appears to be written by someone else (often attorneys or consultants) from the parent's email address, the neutral approach is to treat it as though it is from the parent. The email will likely conform to communication rules, so who sent it is not as important. Obviously, the parent is responsible for anything sent that represents their communication.

Responding as a Neutral Coparent will neither escalate conflict nor yield to something that you find unacceptable. Moreover, if the coparent's new partner is not supposed to have access to that email, then you leave the issue for your coparent to address, rather than inserting yourself into their communication, an action likely to be unwelcomed.

6 When should I ask my coparent for an in-person meeting to talk about a problem?

Most of the coparenting information that needs to be shared is factual and can be communicated by email or text such as these examples:

- "When is the special school activity?"
- "Where is the game being played?"
- "The kids need new sporting equipment."
- "The doctor said it is only a cold and she needs to rest at home from school for a day or two."
- "The kids were in the car when the coparent had an accident, but no one was injured."

A phone call is needed if the child has a medical crisis, such as a trip to the emergency room or involvement in an auto accident in which someone is injured. The death of a grandparent and funeral plans may require phone contact. Discussing how to introduce a new significant other to the children needs an in-person, often professionally supported conversation.

More complex parenting issues likely need to be talked about in detail. For example, the parents will likely need to meet in person if a child is sexually self-stimulating in a way that alarms a parent, the child is suspended from school, or a teacher writes that the child is failing a course. Coparenting issues like these involve high emotions and complex behavior patterns. An Escalated Coparent may hurl challenging questions, with a tone of judgment and blame: "Who is responsible for the problem?"; "What steps were taken to prevent the problem from occurring?"; "Has a parent failed in their duty to monitor the child?" It's also easy for an Escalated Coparent to make demeaning statements such as, "You've never been any good at choosing to sit with them to do homework rather than working on your own computer." An Escalated Coparent may take unilateral action, that is, respond to the problem without reaching out to their coparent. They may call child protective services, or they may arrange a private meeting with the coparent counselor or the child's counselor, rather than requesting a conjoint meeting.

The Neutral Coparent responds in a straightforward, matter-of-fact fashion. Asking for a coparenting business meeting may be best because it signals that an important matter needs to be addressed in a business-like manner with a protocol to be followed. The initiating parent asks to schedule a meeting and provides their available dates and times. The initiating parent identifies the issues they want to discuss so that their coparent can be prepared and not feel ambushed. If you are concerned that talking directly with the coparent will end up in a conversation in which you are attacked, blamed, and frustrated, it is probably best to have a third party involved as a conversational manager, or perhaps a qualified professional who can contribute ideas to the discussion.

How might a parent respond if their coparent is not providing needed information, e.g., times of doctor's appointments, contact information for sports coaches, child's health insurance card?

Your coparent may think that you do not need or are not entitled to the information you are requesting. As a first step, take a look at the divorce decree/parenting plan. Refresh your understanding about each coparent's communication responsibilities. The general rule is that both parents are entitled to information from the school, medical providers, and extracurricular activities that occur during both parents' parenting time, and each parent is responsible to obtain that type of information on their own. The court-ordered parenting plan usually says that when an extracurricular activity, such as piano lessons, occurs only during one parent's time, that parent has no obligation to provide this information to the coparent. The courts recognize that each parent wants to enjoy time with the children without the tension of unnecessary coparenting communication. A Neutral Coparent will offer information about a child's special activities, even though they are not required to do so. They will be guided by best practices, rather than the minimum obligation of information sharing. For example, they could forward notices about special events at the school or special moments the child has with their friends. This is an easy way to make a peace offering.

There are instances when the coparent will not receive information directly from a third-party source (school website, team parent, etc.) and it must come through their coparent, such as what happened at a child's medical appointment.

Out-of-town travel is another instance when information needs to be shared. The parent traveling with the child should provide information about the child's sleeping location each night, contact information the non-custodial parent can use to reach the child, transportation details, and an airline itinerary if air travel is involved. But the parent vacationing with the children is usually not required to disclose the day-to-day schedule of activities for the children or who they will be with. And Neutral Coparents accept that when a parent is on vacation with the children and enjoying a break from their usual responsibilities, they also want to enjoy a break from coparenting tension, so the Neutral Coparent does not get upset if they go several days without talking to the children.

Coparenting conflict escalates when parents do not freely share information about doctor's appointments, extracurricular activities, health insurance information, and the like. An Escalated Coparent may send less than the minimally required information, or they may withhold it. When both parents are escalated, the response may be an angry/threatening text or email, or a parent may, in turn, withhold information. Or, a lawyer may file a court motion alleging contempt and seeking a sanction such as a fine and reimbursement for the cost of bringing the action. Trying to obtain information from your coparent by threat, pressure, or intimidation rarely works. Even when it works, it sets a terrible tone for future interactions.

If an Escalated Coparent is not providing information, the Neutral Coparent could choose to write something such as: "We don't seem to be doing very well at exchanging information in a timely manner. I hope I am not doing anything to make it hard on your end. Can we agree to respond to each other's emails within 24 hours? Or if either of us is too busy to timely respond, then maybe you could respond by saying I will get the needed information in 48 or 72 hours." A diplomatic request like this may need to be repeated several times. If repeated requests do not bring resolution, then the wise response may be for both parents to sit down with a professional to talk about what is going on and what can be done to improve coparenting communication.

How do I keep information about the divorce private so that my child does not have access to it?

There are several strategies a Neutral Coparent could choose to take:

- One of the difficult parts of divorcing is having to tell everyone in the social circle what is happening. Neutral Coparents pick out one or two people to whom they talk candidly and confidentially about what is going on. Everyone else is given carefully edited responses to questions.
- Store legal documents in a locked filing cabinet. Some parents create a separate, password-protected email account for legal documents.
- Prevent the children's access to the parents' computers and any digital communication devices that are used to communicate about the divorce.

- Do not talk about the divorce on the phone with family or friends when the children are at home or in the car (even if the children have earbuds in).
- Do not look at the children's phones to monitor text or emails exchanges between the child and their other parent.
- Do not act on beliefs such as, "The kids have a right to know," or "I never lie to my children." In general, the rule of thumb is that as children grow up, they will naturally figure out on their own what is appropriate for them to know.
- When a Neutral Coparent is emotionally upset about a divorce-related event, they keep it to themselves, or they say to the child something like, "It's okay; the divorce is difficult for us all. I just need a few minutes to rest and then I'll be good to go again."
- Neutral Coparents restrain themselves from correcting a child when the child says something that is factually wrong about the divorce. For example, the child says to Mom, "Dad says you get enough money in child support to pay for my school trip to Washington, D.C." The Neutral Coparent responds by saying something like, "You don't need to know about things like what child support pays for. Sometimes Dad and I don't agree about who is responsible for what expenses. Please don't worry about it. We will work it out as best as we can."

9 My child doesn't get their homework done when they are with their other parent. What can I do?

Coordinating homework between households can spark coparenting conflicts, even when the guidelines of parallel coparenting (see Chapter 14) are being followed.

Let's assume each parent is accessing the school's homework portal to find out when assignments are due. Let's also assume each parent says they are carefully monitoring the children's homework when the children are at their home. Still, homework completion is a problem.

An Escalated Coparent fires off nasty emails or takes one-sided actions to address the problem, such as hiring a tutor or arranging for a parent-teacher meeting without telling the other parent.

A Neutral Coparent communicates with their coparent to make sure they have a shared understanding of what is expected of each of them. They develop a shared strategy for ensuring that test preparation and homework are done.

For coparents who do not communicate well, it can be useful to simply scan and email to the other parent which assignments the child brought home from school and what was completed at the end of the night. This strategy can seem time-consuming, but it provides each parent a complete picture of homework assignments and what came home in the school bag. Of course, kids lose and misplace things, and the dog ate it. But if each parent has a complete record of schoolwork, when something does go wrong, or a completed assignment never makes it to the teacher, it is easier to talk with the child about personal responsibility, rather than the parents fighting about who is more irresponsible and who lost what.

CHAPTER 10

Coparenting Solutions: Responding to Your Child's Complaints

COPARENTING SOLUTIONS: RESPONDING TO YOUR CHILD'S COMPLAINTS

My child says they don't like being with their other parent. How do I respond in a way that shows I respect their feelings without further straining the parent-child relationship?

Good parents are protective. They want to know the source of the strain between their child and coparent; they want to remove the child from a threat. The problem is that the source of the child's resistance is often hotly debated but rarely resolved.

Let's assume that the favored parent is committed to following the court-ordered parenting time schedule. The favored parent wants the child to feel heard; the favored parent wants the child's dislike and discomfort respected and relieved. They typically believe the child's reports more than those of their coparent. At the same time, the favored parent does not want to encourage resistance in the child that may be fallout from the divorce and is not based on the child's actual experience with the other parent.

The favored parent is in a pickle. They want to ask questions so they can more fully understand the child's complaints, but they want to avoid questions that might amplify the child's complaints or contribute to the favored parent's own sense of alarm and powerlessness. Worse, questions may plant ideas in the child's mind, such as these examples: "Do you feel more uncomfortable when Mom is with her friend?" "Are you uncomfortable because Daddy works when you are with him?" "Did you feel safe with Mommy this time?" Then there is the horrible thought that if the child is being mistreated and the favored parent doesn't act, child protective services may take the child away from *them*.

The Neutral Coparent understands they can't really know what is going on at the coparent's home. The Neutral Coparent practices the following kinds of **LEARNS** behaviors:

- **L**istens carefully
- **E**mpathizes that the child's relationship with the resisted parent is hard right now
- **A**ccepts they cannot know what really happens at the coparent's house
- **R**einforces the child's resilience and ability to cope
- **N**ever expresses doubt about the coparent
- **S**upports the child talking directly with the coparent, and if possible, works with their coparent in a collaborative manner to address the child's expressed concerns

11 My coparent remarried and my child says they do not like their new stepparent. They say they want less time at your coparent's home. What do I say?

Children's complaints about new partners are much like lightning during a thunderstorm—pretty likely, though not a sure thing. Stepparents married to a resisted parent are in a nearly impossible spot. If the children are resisting the biological parent, they will almost always resist a stepparent or a new partner. Compounding the problem is that the favored parent often has little trust in the new stepparent and also holds negative beliefs and attitudes, and vice versa. Favored parents tend to accept the child's complaints about the stepparent as adequate proof that something is wrong with the new partner's parenting. A favored parent thinks, "Anyone who would get involved with my ex must have issues."

Stepparents tend to make coparenting conflict either significantly better or significantly worse. They may be the calmer presence in the household, easier to communicate with, and have a slower burning fuse. They may be more diplomatic in responding to a problem that arises and less likely to escalate conflict.

On the other hand, a stepparent may feel the need to carry the banner in battle for their spouse. They, too, are made miserable by the conflict. Intractable conflict tends to isolate opposing sides into tribal warfare. Even stepparents who try to remain neutral usually get drawn into the polarized thinking that frames intractable RRP.

The Neutral Coparent assumes that:

- The stepparent likely wants to stay out of the conflict muck.
- The child is likely having a negative experience with the stepparent because of the child's resistance to their biological parent.
- The child is probably safe with the stepparent.
- The stepparent can be a buffer for the child against the coparenting conflict.

The Neutral Coparent looks to the stepparent as a peacemaker for the family. Tough duty, no doubt. Meeting with the resisted parent and the stepparent takes a lot of courage for the Neutral Coparent. An Escalated Coparent may not allow the stepparent to meet with their coparent; there is nothing a stepparent can do about that. An Escalated Stepparent may not accept that their good intentions are going unheeded and may reach out to the favored parent, an action that will likely provoke the favored parent instead of resulting in a peace initiative.

If a child says they want less time at your coparent's home, the Neutral Coparent says artfully but clearly, "That is not an option." One parent explained to his child that in many families only some family members feel close and enjoy one another; others find a family member difficult to deal with. Some don't like a family member for a while, then later they do. But healthy families don't engage in splits and cutoffs as they journey through life.

Love's way is not easy. You and your coparent can teach your child that love can be hard and love's pain can be deep, but no matter what, you will support your child as they find their way through the difficult side of love.

12 My child complains about the chores they have to do at the resisted parent's home. How do I respond?

Besides death and taxes, one of life's certainties is that a child who has chores will complain to somebody and possibly multiple somebodies. A common polarization occurs when one parent is more permissive and indulges the children while the other parent is more structured and comfortable giving the children consequences when they do not meet their responsibilities. Everyone knows that children prefer to hang out in homes where they have fewer chores, limits, and consequences. Also, children tend to present as victims: "She makes us clean the dishes, clean our bathroom, and pick up dog poop while she's on Facebook."

When a child complains about chores at the coparent's home, the Escalated Parent takes the child at their word and makes another entry in their parenting journal about the outrageous and abusive behavior the children are being subjected to.

The Neutral Coparent could make a gracefully worded inquiry to their coparent about the child's complaint. For example, "George, the kids complained again that at your house they have to do lots of chores. They seem to think they are doing work that you should be doing. Let's not get tripped up on this. What would be helpful for me to know to support you around chores? Do you have a suggestion for how I could respond to them?" The Neutral Coparent could say something to the children like, "You are fortunate that Dad makes you do chores. He is trying to help you learn to be independent and self-reliant. Sometimes I am too soft with you." You could say that you expect them to like or not to like some of the things you do as a parent and some of the parenting practices of their other parent, but in the long run they will benefit from the differences.

The Neutral Coparent encourages the child to voice their concerns directly to the other parent. The problem exists between the child and the coparent, and the Neutral Coparent can reduce the family's conflict by not inserting themselves into the middle of this problem. However, it can be hard for a parent to restrain their desire to shield their child from what the child portrays as unhealthy stress. Finally, the Neutral Coparent accepts the issue as an opportunity to learn more about themselves as a parent, to ask if they need to shut off their worried thoughts more quickly, and to raise their expectations about the children being able to problem-solve for themselves.

13 Should the resisted parent send cards/gifts on special occasions if the child refuses to accept them and says they don't want them?

The resisted parent must be honest with themselves. If he or she behaved poorly—for example, they lost their composure and said to the child, "Fine, if you don't want to be here, I don't want you here!"—the child is likely harboring resentment or maybe even holding a grudge and does not want a peacemaking offer or expression of caring. Contact with the child must start with a statement of regret and responsibility about the offending behavior. If the resistance to the parent is in the mild range, a sincere apology might convince the child that the parent's remorse is genuine and they deserve a second chance.

If the child's resistance is in the moderate to severe range, for whatever reasons, the resisted parent should send cards and small gifts on special occasions, even if the child says they don't want them and refuses to receive them. A child may be explaining to a therapist why they don't want contact with the resisted parent, yet at the same time complain, "And they haven't even tried to contact me." Damned if you do and damned if you don't, right?

Gifts should be more than a token, but far less than something that opens itself to accusations that a parent is trying to buy love or affection. In one case, a mom who had not seen her children for over a year brought four or five gifts for each child to the first reunification session. The children excitedly opened them, but the favored parent refused to take the gifts home, saying they were excessive. A small, meaningful gift can communicate to the child that you remember what is meaningful to them and that you are steadfast in your devotion to them. It can symbolize the special love you have for them in your heart.

While it may be a stretch and not possible in some situations, a Neutral Favored Parent could tell the resisted parent what the child has been asking for, or might otherwise want or appreciate. This can be beneficial for three reasons. One, it provides the best chance the child will respond positively to the gift. Second, if the child knows the only way the resisted parent would know about that gift or item is if the favored parent told them, this communicates to the child that the favored parent does support the relationship with the resisted parent. Third, this kind of dialogue is a powerful peacemaking gesture demonstrating that the favored parent actively supports the child's relationship with the resisted parent. Or, even more of a peacemaking strategy would be for both parents to jointly give the gift, communicating as directly as possible the favored parent's support of the relationship between the resisted parent and the child.

CHAPTER 11

Coparenting Solutions: Responding to Your Child's Resistance

COPARENTING SOLUTIONS: RESPONDING TO YOUR CHILD'S RESISTANCE

My child says they won't go to their other parent's anymore for parenting time regardless of what the court says. How do I respond?

Let's suppose the following scenario: the favored parent wants the child to have a relationship with the resisted parent. Also, assume the child gets anxious when it is time for parenting time with the resisted parent. Finally, assume the favored parent and the child have had several conversations about the basis for the child's resistance, so talking about it more is not the issue now.

The Escalated Coparent allows their anxiety about the child's well-being, and their belief that the child should be able to choose where they spend their time, to trump the importance of the child learning to cope with difficult relationships. The Escalated Parent may think it is more important to protect their relationship with the child than to risk the child's pushback if the parent insists on compliance with the court's orders. If the Escalated Parent allows the child to deviate from the court-ordered plan, they teach the child that asserting personal desires is more important than obeying court orders. The Escalated Coparent says to the child, "I want you to have a relationship with your mom if you want to," or "when you're ready," or "when you're comfortable." Or the Escalated Coparent says, "Ok, I will talk to my attorney about it." Responses like these may arise from the natural instinct to protect a child, but they are misguided and do not promote healthy child development. As an alternative, the favored parent could offer to get an attorney for the child with the understanding that until the court's orders are changed, the child must comply with them.

The Neutral Coparent understands that, as the favored parent, their relationship with the child is very close and positive. They know what they say to the child has persuasive power. The Neutral Coparent has a heart-to-heart talk with the child. The Neutral Coparent tells the child how important it is to address and work through their problems with the resisted coparent, as opposed to avoiding them, which only ensures that they remain unresolved. The Neutral Coparent says, "In this family, we obey rules, laws, and court orders. If I think the court order needs to be changed, I will start that process, but in the meantime, we have to follow the plan ordered by the court." They may point out that the courts want the child to "have a voice"; that is, the court will consider the child's opinions and wishes about the parenting schedule, but having a voice is not the same as the same as making the choice. The Neutral Coparent recognizes that it is normal for a child to express resistance to various requirements placed on them, such as earning good grades in school, turning off the computer and coming to the dinner table, or picking up their room. But when the child's naturally occurring resistance severs the relationship with a loving parent, the child's resistance has gone from healthy expression of emerging independence to unhealthy coping.[34]

It takes a lot of life experience to take on the responsibility of defining the family's legacy. The risk is quite high that if the child defies the court's order and cuts off contact with the resisted parent, the problem will get a lot worse before it gets better (if it ever gets better). The Neutral Coparent listens to and empathizes with the child's concerns, and encourages the child to discuss these with the resisted parent (or with the professional who is supporting the parent-child relationship). Perhaps the Neutral Coparent even offers to meet with the child and the resisted coparent, or suggests a professional intervene with the family issue. The Neutral Coparent may need to emphasize that the level of conflict in the family is unacceptable and dangerous to everyone's health and well-being. The Neutral Coparent remains firm that the child is going to spend time with the other parent and is clear the child will have consequences if they refuse to go, such as loss of access to electronic devices. Finally, the Neutral Coparent advises the resisted coparent of what is going on and appeals to them to work together on the issue.

15 My child says they will run away, harm themselves, or commit suicide if forced to go to their other parent's home. How do I respond?

A child making statements like these is a matter for genuine alarm. The Escalated Coparent may overestimate the severity of the threat. They may believe they are obligated to act with an abundance of caution, and thus conclude their duty is to withhold the child and prevent parenting time with the resisted parent until they are confident the child is not at risk. The Escalated Coparent may argue that the child's threat of self-harm is a sure sign the child is endangered or severely traumatized when in their coparent's care. They may insist reunification with the coparent needs to be halted because it is too disruptive to the child's overall well-being.

The resisted parent may react to this situation in such a way to further escalate the conflict and the problem. They may call the police to enforce the court's order. And if the police do not enforce the order, the resisted parent may have little choice other than initiating a court action to enforce parenting time, alleging they have been victimized by an alienating coparent. While the slow wheels of justice are grinding, the child won't have contact with the resisted parent. And, by the time the case is heard, the parents will be deeply aggravated with each other, and the child will think they don't have to go if they don't want to. At this point, it will also be a lot harder to reconcile the relationship between the child and their resisted parent, and several bank accounts will have been depleted in the process.

The resisted parent may react by not pursuing reunification or by counter-rejecting the child. They may say something like, "If you feel that strongly about not seeing me, then fine. Call when you feel differently." The difficulty is that it is not uncommon for there to be a disconnect between what the child is saying/insisting on and what they truly want. Although the child says they don't want contact, they often feel abandoned if the resisted parent does not try to keep the relationship going. For example, let's say a child refuses contact with a parent for more than a year. Then the child points out that the resisted parent's failure to contact them on their birthday is more proof that the parent doesn't care, so the child is justified in resisting contact.

When the child makes a threat of self-harm, the Neutral Coparent offers emotional support to the child. Then, the Neutral Coparent calls their coparent in the child's presence, preferably on a speaker phone, and briefs their coparent in the most matter-of-fact way they can muster. At the beginning and end of the conversation, the Neutral Coparent states clearly in the child's presence that both parents care about the child, are dedicated to the child's safety and well-being, and will work together to those ends.

Neutral Coparents shift easily into crisis management mode. They know that the first order of business is to assess the level of threat. If coparents do not agree on the nature and severity of the threat, or if they cannot rally their most mature selves to problem-solve the crisis, they need to involve a crisis team to obtain a professional assessment and treatment plan. Children need to know that any threats to harm themselves or others will be taken seriously and acted upon.

16 My child refuses to get in the car to go to the resisted parent's home. What should I do?

Escalated Coparents say to themselves, "It's my coparent's problem. I didn't cause it. It's not my responsibility to fix it. She brought it on herself, and I get it why my child feels this way." This is being passive-aggressive, that is, expressing one's anger by not doing anything. The Escalated Coparent may say in an aggravated tone, "What do you expect me to do, force my child into the car? They are too big for that, and besides I won't do it. It's negatively impacting my own relationship with my child." Or, they may say in a nonchalant tone, "Maybe the best thing to do is to let my coparent (or child) have some time without contact. We shouldn't force the issue." And the Escalated Parent does not give the child a consequence for not going, which is sure to increase the child's resistance. They tell the child that not respecting the authority of the court order is okay. This sends a message to the child that their relationship with the resisted parent is less important than any of the other responsibilities the favored parent would insist the child perform, such as going to school, doing homework, going to the doctor, or going to boring dinners with extended family.

The Neutral Coparent calms the child, talks with the child about their concerns, and calls the coparent to give them a heads-up that the situation is dicey. If the child is unable to calm themselves, or gets stubborn and refuses to calm themselves, a fallback plan is to tell the child that they don't have to go to the resisted parent's home, but they are not allowed to stay with the favored parent. Instead, they will spend the time of the court-ordered parenting schedule at another adult's home (not their best friend's), without their electronics and without access to social media or their friends. Additionally, they will receive similar consequences when they return to the favored parent's home for disrespecting both parents and the court's orders.

The Neutral Coparent has a heart-to-heart talk with the child and shares their convictions about how important it is for the child to have regular contact and relationships with both parents and both sides of the family. They may say the family is going through a transition that is uncomfortable, uncertain, and anxiety-provoking, but necessary. The Neutral Coparent expresses their own personal regret to the child for contributing to a situation the child finds so difficult. The child's anguish is a family problem. The family has to rally and find a peaceable way to live, even though that may seem impossible or hopeless at the time.

When the family crisis has escalated to these proportions, Neutral Coparents seek the assistance of a behavioral health professional or another neutral third party. With the assistance of a third party, the coparents negotiate a plan for making parenting time exchanges quickly and as stress free as possible. They may agree upon consequences for the child if the child refuses or contacts the favored parent in distress during the other parent's access time, begging to come "home." The coparents then meet together with the child to explain their plan and to demonstrate they are going to work together as coparents to make the parenting plan work for the child. They explain to the child the agreements they have reached about what everyone will do to get the parenting time plan back on track, and what the consequences are if the child refuses to cooperate with the parenting plan.

Pro tip for the resisted parent: while the exchange is occurring, don't interfere with the favored parent working with the child who is resisting the transition; just sit and watch. Take the opportunity to thank your coparent for their efforts.

17 When my coparent calls or texts, my child doesn't want to communicate with them. How should I handle this?

Telephone or digital contact with the non-custodial parent is a common problem among dual-household families, even when RRP is not occurring. Family routines are busy. Dinner is happening. The kids are at an activity or in the bathtub. Everyone is in the car where there is no privacy. Even when a custodial parent makes it a priority for the child to communicate with the non-custodial parent, it is hard to get it to happen reliably. Our experience is that even with coparents who are operating in cooperative or parallel coparenting models, about 10 to 20 percent of the non-custodial parent's attempts for phone and digital contact do not work on any given day. That is to say, coparents should not get upset when every contact doesn't happen.

In families with RRP, contact by the non-custodial parent is more often problematic. An Escalated Coparent who has the children doesn't check voicemail and ensure the other parent's calls are returned in a timely manner (for example, before bedtime or first thing the next morning). Or, when the call comes in, they say, "Your mom is calling," and thus allow the child to decide if they want to talk to their other parent. The Escalated Coparent may use a sour tone or expression when the phone rings and say, "It's him." They don't ensure the child has privacy for the call, or they put the call on speakerphone. They don't insist the child practice common phone etiquette and stop watching a video when the other parent is trying to get a conversation started with the child. Or, if the call with the other parent lasts a long time, they pester the child to finish the call. If the child is talking to the coparent and becoming emotional, the Escalated Coparent may feel annoyed with the non-custodial parent, believing that their parenting time is being compromised, and take the phone from the child and hang up.

An Escalated Coparent initiating the call may fuel conflict escalation by sending multiple text messages to the custodial parent if their call is not answered when they expect. Or, they may argue that they should be allowed to purchase a phone for the child to take with them to the other parent's home, to ensure they can reach the child without having to go through the custodial parent. They send the custodial parent highlighted billing records showing how often they tried to call and did not receive a response. Or, they keep the child on the phone for a long time.

We recommend calls from the non-custodial parent last no more than five to 10 minutes per child maximum. The most meaningful part of the call from the non-custodial parent occurs during the first few minutes when the effort to make the connection communicates commitment and affection (I love you; I'm thinking of you).

When frequent coparenting conflict is present, it may be wise to limit communication with the non-custodial parent to days when the non-custodial parent and child would not otherwise have contact. That is, if the non-custodial parent dropped off the child for school in the morning, contact later in the day is unnecessary. Because family schedules are busy and often fluctuate, the Neutral Coparent may define a window of time for the non-custodial parent's call, for example, between 6:30 p.m. and 7:30 p.m.

Scheduling calls is particularly important when the child is away on an extended vacation. The timing of calls should be worked out before vacation starts. A Neutral Coparent appreciates that especially during vacations, custodial parents want to have the children to themselves with minimum coparenting tension, so they do not insist on daily contact. A call every other day or every third day is reasonable contact in most cases. The traveling coparent agrees to initiate the call to ensure they occur during a time that is not so disruptive to vacation fun. They understand it may be hard for the non-custodial parent to get the children talking in a meaningful way on the phone, especially with a resisted parent. So, a Neutral Favored Parent encourages the kids to think ahead of time about the best things that happened to them that day during the vacation so they will have something to tell the other parent when they call.

The child's phone or text communication with the favored parent during the resisted parent's family time can be a hot-button topic. The resisted parent may say, "The kids do fine at my house until their mother calls. Then they get moody again." Or, "They stay in their rooms texting the other parent all day." Neutral Coparents may forge an agreement that the favored parent will not let the kids complain about what is happening at the resisted parent's home. In more extreme situations—when contact with the favored parents becomes an ongoing sore point, or the moodiness of the child after talking with the favored parent disrupts the resisted parent's quality time with the child—coparents should consider eliminating the non-custodial, favored parent's telephone contact and minimizing text contact. Also, Neutral Coparents never tell the children to delete text messages that they send to the child so that the coparent cannot read them.

18 My child says they are totally miserable at their other parent's house. What should I do?

It is possible that the child says the same thing in both households. The child may miss having an intact family more than anything else. The child may say they are miserable when they are with the resisted parent, but they don't act that way with that parent. Neutral Coparents will talk about their respective parenting time experiences to see if there is an actual issue or if it's just something that the child needs to work out on their own.

In families with RRP, inconsistencies between the child's actual experience and reports about their experience in their two homes is common and often a source of conflict. The favored parent may think their coparent is minimizing what is going on, or that the child is miserable but afraid to show or talk about it with that parent. An Escalated Coparent takes the child's reports as gospel truth, as confirmation that the other parent treats the child as terribly as the other parent treated the Escalated Coparent during their intimate relationship. When the child returns to their home, the Escalated Coparent makes special time to talk with the child about what happened during the visit with the resisted parent. This talk may take on the tone of a ritual or a tradition or in the extreme, an interrogation. The favored, Escalated Parent may think such talks show they have special closeness with the child because the child will share with them openly what they will not share with the resisted parent. Escalated Coparents become alarmed about what they hear; they let their protective instincts loose. They don't want to accept that their attentive listening to the child's complaints may amplify them. They don't realize their attentive listening suggests to the child that they want to hear more complaints. Or, that the child may be getting the impression that the attentive parent may do something to intervene on the child's behalf, suggesting to the child that if they complain more, they will get more control over the parenting time schedule.

A Neutral Coparent learns to manage the anxiety they feel when the child reports that they are unhappy. The Escalated Coparent may find it hard not to join the child by expressing their own sadness and worry about the divorce and the child's discomfort and well-being. A Neutral Coparent doesn't share such feelings and beliefs, or even let on that they are feeling concerned. They may tell the child that if the child complains about their other parent's home, the Neutral Coparent will need to talk with their coparent to get their point of view. They tell the child they are in a bind because they were not there. They say the information they have about the coparent is not entirely consistent with what the child is saying, so they don't know what the truth is, and they don't know who to believe about what. They explain to the child they do not have control over what happens in the other parent's home, and this is the way it needs to be. They say they are confident the child can work it out with their other parent. They encourage the child to be creative and find ways to enjoy their time in the other parent's home, while recognizing it is difficult for them at this point in time.

If these strategies do not help to ease the complaints, consider having the child work with a counselor to improve the child's readiness and skillfulness for problem-solving with the resisted parent. Both parents should consult with the counselor to seek guidance on how to best respond.

19 When my child comes to my home, they refuse to come out of their room and join us for meals. What should I do?

A child refusing to join the family for dinner is upsetting and may even feel insulting, but a parent should think carefully about what issues may be contributing to the problem. For example, who is at the table and what is being served can make a difference. If a new partner or stepparent is seated at the table with their children, initiating a new ritual for family mealtime can be challenging for the child. It may take a few weeks or months before the child is ready to relax their resistance, so the solution may be to patiently wait until the child is ready. A Neutral Coparent uses the minimal amount of parenting authority necessary to get the child to behave in their home.

Let's assume the child's refusal to join the family for dinner is their way of expressing anger toward the resisted parent. A child's defiance can be thought of as occurring at three levels of severity. At level one, you can talk with the child and come to a mutually agreeable approach to the issue. At level two, a verbal approach will not work, and a behavioral consequence is necessary, such as loss of access to electronics. At level three, the child is so upset they are unable to be reasonable or rational and may need a referral to counseling.

If one parent misreads the level of the child's distress, this parent can escalate the conflict in the parent-child relationship. The parent may get angry with the child for not talking; the parent responds with threats or demands. If the parent takes away electronics and the child does not really seem to care, the child will dig in a little deeper against the parent. If the child's refusal is level three defiance, seeking the support of the favored parent or a mental health professional may be the best option.

The favored parent encouraging the child to move beyond their anger is an example of a favored parent acting to reduce the impact of conflict on the family. If the favored parent is in escalation mode, they will refuse to help. If the favored parent is in neutral mode, they will talk with the resisted parent about options. Is there an activity the resisted coparent can offer that will result in the child eating with the family outside the house? Are there gradual approaches to the problem both parents can support, such as allowing the child to eat in their room some days only, if they agree to help with cleanup? Or, the favored parent may agree to talk with the child to make clear the many reasons they do not approve of the child expressing their conflicted feelings by freezing what should be a central symbol of family warmth. If the child does not seem to have the resources to deal with their relationship problems more directly, the parents may agree that counseling is needed, and in a unified voice present this option to the child.

Perhaps there is a simple approach to the problem, such as a cereal that the child can prepare themselves, as an alternative to eating what everyone else at the table is having. A Neutral Coparent is firm in some fundamental ways, yet flexible in others that are less critical. Asking one's coparent for advice about preferred diet and dinner routines in a respectful, appreciative way can be helpful in these situations.

20 My child refuses to have contact with my coparent's extended family. What should I do?

The Escalated Coparent does nothing. If they think RRP is not their responsibility or concern, they do not feel the need to support those relationships. The Escalated Coparent thinks nothing of his or her own uncaring attitude. It doesn't bother them that they now feel cold and indifferent about people they know well and with whom they once had a decent and meaningful relationship. They wouldn't give a second thought to stories of adults who lost family relationships as children and later grieve the magnitude of their loss. They may appreciate the richness relationship with grandparents can bring to a child, but in their resentment toward the resisted parent, they are comfortable to sacrifice those relationships as well.

The Escalated Coparent does not flex the schedule to accommodate visits from out-of-town relatives or for family reunions. In more severe cases, the Escalated Coparent does not allow the child to attend the funeral of an aunt, uncle, or grandparent.

Sometimes an Escalated Coparent forms an alliance with a member of the coparent's extended family or with their former spouse that is based on mutual anger toward the other parent. Doing so is certain to reinforce negative beliefs about the excluded parent and result in the child's increased resistance.

A Neutral Coparent understands that peacemaking means acting to support the interests of the coparent, and that supporting the child's relationship with the coparent's extended family is a powerful peacemaking gesture. A Neutral Coparent may stay in touch with their coparent's extended family to ensure the child has time with that side of the family, even if they do not have contact with their resisted parent. A Neutral Coparent may send pictures of the child to extended family, include them on holiday gift and card lists, and arrange telephone contact with them. Assisting in maintaining a relationship with the extended family can provide an important bridge or stepping stone toward repairing the child's contact and relationship with the resisted parent.

21 What can I do if my child refuses to open gifts and cards sent by my coparent and members of their extended family?

Gifts and cards from a resisted parent and their family are peacemaking gestures. An Escalated Coparent does not tell the child the gifts have arrived. They may give the gifts away to a charity or tell the child that the parent didn't care enough to remember their special event. More often, the Escalated Coparent gives the child the gift but fails to use the gift-giving to encourage peacemaking. For example, a Neutral Coparent might tell the child that the gift shows that the resisted parent truly and deeply cares about them.

A Neutral Coparent uses gifting as a teaching moment to teach the child about developing appropriate compassion and generosity, even when one feels hurt, angry, and spiteful. A Neutral Coparent does not guilt or force the child to open the presents or respond to a card, but the parent may ask the child to listen as they share their wisdom about the difference between standing up for oneself versus being mean. Or, a Neutral Coparent may ask the child to open the gift from the resisted parent before they open other gifts as a way of emphasizing how important family is, no matter what shape the family is in.

A Neutral Coparent may share with the child teachings about forgiveness from the religion they practice. They may point out to the child that all religions value forgiveness. That family is where some of the most gut-wrenching life lessons are learned, including the deepest and most inspiring lessons about intimate relationships and love.

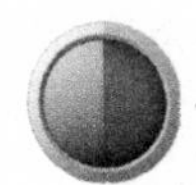

CAUTION: The term *forgiveness* can be off-putting to a disgruntled parent or angry child because it may be viewed to mean something like a pardon for a bad deed. Forgiveness is about achieving internal peace regardless of how one was injured. Forgiveness is closer to being merciful than it is to wiping the slate clean. A Neutral Coparent can share stories or online videos about extraordinary acts of forgiveness, for example, "How to Forgive When It Still Hurts," https://youtu.be/pdMnilwB_d8.

CHAPTER 12

Coparenting Solutions: Talking to Your Child About Their Other Parent

COPARENTING SOLUTIONS: TALKING TO YOUR CHILD ABOUT THEIR OTHER PARENT

22 How do I ask my child about what they did during their time with their other parent?

A parenting workshop leader referred to teenagers at the dinner table as "mopheads," that is, they look down and away from you, so the parent directs questions to the top of the child's head—hence, mopheads. Getting children to talk—whether they're teenagers or not—about what happened at the coparent's home may be doubly hard. They may not be in a talkative mood, and certainly not in the mood to talk about a topic that makes them feel ill at ease, such as their relationship with their other parent. It's awkward when a topic so important can feel taboo. The kids know a lot about this person you used to know most everything about; now you are curious but not allowed to ask, and they may not be allowed to talk.

The Neutral Coparent lives by the wise saying, "Strong fences make good neighbors." They respect the importance of boundaries in relationships. A Neutral Coparent asks general, positive questions such as, "What were the highlights of your time with Mom?" Examples of other appropriate questions are:

- "Did you bring your homework with you?"
- "What progress did you make on your project?"
- "How did your sports practices go?"
- "What are some of the things you like doing at Mom's house that I can do here?"
- "Dad's birthday is coming up; let's think about a way of sending him a nice birthday wish."

- "Do you have something to give your mother for Mother's Day? If not, want me to help you?"
- "Even though my home is Islamic and Mom is Christian, I'm curious to know how you are going to celebrate the holiday."
- Tell me about something nice your mom did for you last weekend.
- Have you gotten anything new and fun for your bedroom at Dad's?

These kinds of questions support the child's positive regard and affection for your coparent and show you value their contribution to raising your child.

When thinking about questions to ask about the coparent's home, Neutral Coparents use a variation of "the headline test"; that is, what would the coparent think about my question if they were to see a video of me asking it? Neutral Coparents appreciate that in the long run reducing tension and conflict serves the best interests of the children. They understand that reducing conflict means knowing less about the child's life while they are in the coparent's home. This is sad, and perhaps does not seem acceptable. However, exposing the child to coparenting conflict is toxic for the child, and asking questions about problems in the other parent's home can put the child in the middle of conflict. If a Neutral Coparent is anxious about what is happening to the child in the coparent's home, they talk with another adult or a counselor until their anxiety is reduced and they are back in their comfort zone. When they do not feel internal pressure, they could contact the coparent directly (email or phone, not during a parenting time exchange) and ask for clarification, but they should not ask the child.

What are examples of questions parents should avoid asking children about their time at their other parent's?

Nature instilled in parents a fierce desire to protect their offspring. When they sense their child is in danger or needs emotional soothing, a mighty urge arises to spring into protective action. Some moms describe themselves as being a "Momma bear," which hints at the fierce urge they feel to protect their cubs. When a parent perceives the child to be at risk with the other parent, staying "neutral" can be really difficult. Divorced parents usually have leftover concerns from the marriage about the coparent's behavior patterns that could serve as smoldering ashes to ignite worries triggered by the child's reports about the other parent.

An Escalated Coparent may believe their parental rights include access to certain kinds of information, such as the names and addresses of childcare providers. They may believe that if the information is not offered to them, they are entitled to ask the child about it. If an Escalated Coparent believes the coparent is making alienating statements about them, they may ask the child leading questions such as:

- "Did you get along with your mom this time?"
- "Did you have trouble sleeping again?"
- "Did Dad go through your backpack to see if you did all your homework?"
- "Did you talk with Mom about changing what she packs in your lunch?"
- "Does Dad understand how you feel about your stepmom?"
- "Did Mom drink wine when you were there?"
- "Did you hang out with Mom, or was she on Facebook again?"
- "You look sad today. Did something happen?"
- "Did Dad tell you I tried to call you twice last night?"

- "Did Mom make you wear those clothes?"
- "You don't have your new (phone, laptop, game, soccer ball, etc.). Wouldn't Dad let you bring it?"
- "What did Mom say about bringing the dog with you next time?"
- "Who is Dad's new girlfriend?"
- "Does your dad ever do anything fun with you?"
- "Dad seems to take you to a lot of activities. Does he ever give you a chance to rest?"
- "How much screen time does Mom let you have?"
- "Do you miss me as much as I miss you?"
- "Did you feel safe at Dad's this time?"
- "Who usually gets up first on school mornings, you or Mom?"

Questions like these put a child squarely in the middle of the parents' conflict. They can distress the child and can contribute to a child's resisting behavior or irrational thinking. They put pressure on the child to give the favored parent the answer they want to hear, and to withdraw from a resisted parent who asks such questions. These kinds of questions nudge the child toward polarized thinking and resentment.

What if my child comes home and says something really concerning such as, "Daddy likes me to sit on his lap and play horsey." What should I say to the child to find out what is happening?

A child engaging in any form of sexually inappropriate talk or behavior statement is concerning, and may make a parent wonder if a crisis is at hand. If sexual misconduct was a problem during the marriage—for example, credit card records showed that Dad was using escort services or going to strip clubs while on business trips or secretly keeping a library of pornographic videos—Mom's alarm might sound full blast.

An Escalated Coparent may ask questions such as: "Did you tell Daddy to stop?" "Did you tell Daddy that was bad?" "How does Daddy touch you while you are playing horsey?" "Did Daddy touch you in a way that made you feel uncomfortable?" If a parent asks leading questions, the parent may end up concluding the coparent was sexually inappropriate with the child instead of simply playing a game. Parents' vulnerability to negative confirmation bias, combined with exposure to news stories about sexual misconduct, makes worries about sexual misconduct a slippery slope leading toward a high-stakes conflict. Sometimes a parent will discuss their worry with a stepparent, grandparent, or other childcare provider, and this person will ask the child questions. If the police or courts become involved, experts may conclude that the truth of what the child is saying is unclear because of the leading questions to which the child was exposed.

Neutral Coparents stick to simple, basic questions. For example, a parent could say to the child, "You know how stories have a beginning, a middle, and an end? I'd like you to start at the beginning and tell me what happened. Beyond broad, open-ended questions like these, the parent should arrange for the child to be seen by their pediatrician or a counselor trained in interviewing children about sexual assaults.

25 I worry that my coparent grills my child about what happens at my house. What can I do about that?

The impact of divorce is loss of family time, closeness, and connection with one's children. When coparenting conflict is high, the flow of information between the homes is reduced to a trickle or is completely nonexistent. A parent who is worried about the well-being of their child and lacks information tends to fill in the information gap with thoughts that exaggerate the likelihood that the child is unhappy, unsafe, or at risk of harm.

Escalated Coparents tend to confuse the intensity of their own feelings with the likelihood that their fears are accurate. They think it is critical to ask the child about what they fear. They tend to give too much credibility to the child's reports and tend to believe the child rather than their coparent.

Sometimes Escalated Coparents develop a pattern of talking intimately with the child after parenting time exchanges. The talks highlight moments of discomfort for the child. The Escalated Coparent prides themselves on how close they are to the child, and how the child will open up to them. A warm, nurturing feeling develops as the parent comforts the child and offers advice about how to cope with the coparent's inadequacies. But the child likes the attention of the Escalated Parent and often provides the Escalated Parent negatively biased reports. The parent may feel such closeness to the child during these conversations that the parent concludes, "My child would not lie to me about this."

Sometimes the Escalated Coparent makes an audio or video recording of their conversation with the child without the child knowing. Or, they share their worries with the grandmother who then asks the child investigative-type questions. Typically, the Escalated Coparent does little to "check the facts" or ask for information that would disconfirm the child's reports.

Neutral Coparents reduce their worry about what happens in the coparent's home by self-soothing or by seeking the support of others to help them see how their worry may be fear-driven and not fact-based. They discourage the child from gossiping and saying critical things about the other parent behind their back that they would be unwilling to say to their face. When a Neutral Coparent concludes that a report from the child needs to be investigated, they write a carefully worded email that says something like this:

"After our recent parenting exchange, Rashid again started complaining you raise your voice a lot and that he is scared to talk to you. I appreciate I do not know what actually happens at your house, and recognize we don't want to stick our noses into each other's business, but since Rashid has brought this up several times, I thought it best that I give you a heads-up. And I admit that I would like to hear from you about what he is saying."

Here is a second example:

"George, I have a question. I don't want to pry into your business, but you know how it is with kids—they say things, and it would help me know what is really going on. The kids make it sound like you worry about what is happening at my house, so you ask them a lot of questions. If this is the case, please let me know. If it is, I think it would be better if you could ask me directly about concerns, and I promise I'll be honest about my responses."

With younger children, some parents exchange a weekly child report in which they brief the coparent on selected topics such as school and homework updates, physical health issues (sleep, diet, and hygiene concerns), unusual behavior, injuries, or family events in which the child participated.

26 I worry that my coparent becomes intoxicated around my child. How do I ask my child about this?

Let's assume that based on history, there is an ongoing concern the coparent has a problem with alcohol consumption, and sometimes they drink irresponsibly when the children are with them. An Escalated Coparent may ask the child questions such as:

- "How many beers did Daddy drink?"
- "Did you feel uncomfortable because Mommy drank wine again?"
- "Does Dad still go into the garage or backyard for a long time?"
- "Did Daddy stay out late again with friends?"
- "Did Mommy go out with her party girlfriends again?"
- "Did your stepdad fall asleep again right after dinner?"
- "Did the house smell funny last weekend?"
- "How many beers are in the refrigerator at Dad's house?"

A Neutral Coparent doesn't ask the child about this issue. They appreciate that putting the child in the middle is short-sighted and could lead to an accusation that they are asking the child to spy for them. If the child comes home and reports an alarming incident, such as, "Mommy got in an accident in the car again," or "Daddy talks funny after he drinks wine with dinner," a Neutral Coparent could ask some open-ended questions that avoid the insinuation that something wrong happened. For example, "What happened when the accident happened with Mommy's car?" "Can you imitate what Daddy sounds like when he talks funny?" "Where were you when these things happened?" "Was anyone else there when this happened?" "What happened next?"

Parents who have substance use disorders sometimes make poor judgments. In one family, a parent was convicted of driving while intoxicated and ordered to use an interlock device on their car's ignition. (Before the car will start, the parent must breathe into the device; if alcohol is detected, the vehicle will not start.) About three months after the interlock device was installed, the child said to the coparent, "Mommy said that she had a sore throat and that I needed to blow into her machine for her." A Neutral Coparent would tell the child that Mommy made a poor choice, and they are not allowed to blow into Mommy's device. A Neutral Coparent would notify the coparent of what the child said, as well as officials involved with the family including attorneys, custody evaluators, probation officers, and the court. Notifying officials and professionals is the best way to investigate serious concerns and obtain reassurance that the child is being protected against risk.

My child says their other parent said mean or sarcastic things about me. What do I do?

Most parents have had heated arguments with one another in which some pretty awful things are said, especially as their intimate relationship is falling apart. The parents we work with tend to remember nasty things their coparent said, so when a child tells one parent the other parent said something mean, old wounds reopen, and it is easy to believe the child. There are two sides to every story, however, and kids gossip. It may seem harsh to say that kids gossip, but would they make the same statement directly to the coparent that they are making behind their back?

An Escalated Coparent may adopt the attitude that "my child does not lie." Though the child may not "lie," they may tell a version of what happened that is self-serving. They may intentionally or unintentionally omit important details, or say something they think the parent would like to hear. Remember, in order to get their way, all children sometimes play one parent against the other. And, children in divorced families have loyalty conflicts that can make a big difference in the information they provide to each parent.

A Neutral Coparent takes what the child says as likely being incomplete, taken out of context or possibly distorted. A Neutral Coparent may tell the child something like, "Every story has a beginning, middle, and end. Tell me everything that happened, starting at the beginning, that led up to Mom/Dad being upset and saying something like that."

Once you get a fuller understanding from the child about what happened, it may not seem like a problem. If it does though, to take stress off the child, the Neutral Coparent could say something like, "It's okay. Dad only says something like that because he's hurting." Or, "Sometimes when parents are angry they say things they don't mean." The Neutral Coparent could write the coparent to report what the child said and request clarification, since they don't know if what the child said is accurate but are concerned. Hopefully, the coparent will provide details that seem believable and reframe the child's report into "the stuff kids say." Or, the coparent's response may be to talk about a behavior problem with the child that occurs at both households, perhaps leading to a shared coparenting strategy.

When my child is with my coparent, they are not allowed to use their smartphone. They can't communicate with their friends or access their schoolwork. I worry they won't be able to call someone in an emergency. What can I do?

An Escalated Coparent criticizes their coparent for being overcontrolling. An Escalated Coparent is quick to call the police when they feel alarmed that the child's well-being may be endangered, or they call a neighbor and ask them to "drop in" on the child, or maybe they themselves drive by the coparent's house. An Escalated Coparent devises an "emergency escape plan" they have developed secretly with the child to use if they feel unsafe with the other parent. An Escalated Coparent may allow the child to sneak phone calls or texts to them after the child is supposed to be in bed asleep.

A Neutral Coparent presumes their coparent does a good enough job of directing the everyday behavior of the child unless they have a lot of factual evidence showing otherwise. A favored Neutral Coparent accepts that contacting the child at their resisted parent's home can stir up the child's resistance. Most parents consider access to a smartphone as a privilege a child earns. Neutral Coparents inform one another about smartphone rules that address the amount of screen time allowed, if the phone's access is restricted, or if they inspect the phone's digital history from time to time.

My child has come to believe horrible, slanderous things about me. How do I tell them the truth about what happened?

This is a very tough problem for the resisted parent. They cringe if their child falsely accuses them of being physically, sexually, or financially abusive. The parent feels betrayed if the child says they never had a good relationship with them, or that the parent didn't provide childcare prior to the family's separation.

An Escalated Resisted Coparent tries to tell their version of the family history to the child and may even argue with the child about who is telling the truth. Believing they are the victims of alienation, the Escalated Coparent may show the child text messages or other documents to prove the favored parent has lied to the child. The classic mistake is to tell the child they have been "brainwashed" by the favored parent, or that they sound just like their favored parent. An Escalated Coparent may argue that they must challenge each statement the child makes that falsely characterizes them, or the child's false belief will become cemented into their brain.

A Neutral Favored Coparent accepts that in the short run there is little they can do to change the child's beliefs because they are rooted in the three Dementors discussed in Chapter 8: polarized thinking, negative confirmation bias, and deep resentment. A Neutral Resisted

Coparent could say something like this: "You are old enough to know that human memory is not like a video-recording. It's more subjective than that. So, what you remember and what I remember may differ quite a bit. I don't want to fight you about that. I want to fight for us to have a better future. I want to show you that after all we have been through, I am not the kind of person who would abuse you or allow you to be hurt. I want to show you that you are safe with me. I want to talk about your fears about my not being a good or trustworthy person. I want to talk about what we can do to make you feel less anxious when you are with me, and what steps you think I can take to prove to you that I am doing what I can to be a good parent for you."

When the reunification process is well under way, the favored parent may be willing to talk to the child and help them develop a more mature understanding of the terrible family conflict that resulted in highly stereotyped, and even demonized views of some family members. The coparents may be able to sit down together and present to the child a new family narrative about the divorce. In the new family story, each parent acknowledges that the divorce was awful for everyone and that they both contributed to the conflict and the resulting problems.

CHAPTER 13

Coparenting Solutions: Supporting Your Anxious Child

COPARENTING SOLUTIONS: SUPPORTING YOUR ANXIOUS CHILD

As the time approaches for a parenting time exchange, my child regularly complains of stomach aches or headaches. Does that mean my child is getting sick because they go to my coparent's home? If going to their other parents is making them sick, shouldn't I keep them home?

Let's assume a pediatrician examines your child and concludes the child's symptoms are stress related. Perhaps the doctor views the symptoms as serious enough that they refer the child to counseling. If the counselor is familiar with RRP, counseling can bring clarity and relief.

If the symptoms occur only prior to parenting time exchanges, an obvious worry is that something very stressful is happening at the coparent's home. The mind of an Escalated Coparent is filled with suspicious thoughts such as, "I knew he wouldn't be able to handle the kids when I wasn't there. He was a lousy husband, and now he is a lousy single dad."

The Escalated Coparent blames the other parent instead of trying to think of more neutral explanations. Maybe the child is testing to see if they have to go when they aren't in the mood. It is no secret that a child may say, "Mom, I feel sick. Can I stay home from school today?" because it is Monday morning, or they haven't done their homework. The Escalated Coparent's mind is not filled with thoughts such as, "I feel so bad that the kids are struggling, but he's their dad and no matter what, they have to have a relationship with him." Rather, they let their wish to protect the children from discomfort, or their belief that the child has a right to decide, to override the importance of the child's relationship with the other parent. They tend to think, "He is not able to care for a sick child."

Professionals who work with RRP sometimes find it hard to identify where a child's resistance is coming from. For example, if the child had a fairly good relationship with the resisted parent prior to the separation, and an evaluator obtained data from multiple sources indicating the resisted parent's parenting skills have been good, yet the child is absolutely refusing to see the parent, the source of the resistance is not obvious. The favored parent has a for-sure answer: the evaluator is missing the point and is just not seeing the severity of the parenting deficits in the resisted parent. The resisted parent has a for-sure answer: the favored parent is alienating the kids. But neither parent is considering the possibility that the coparenting conflict is the root of the problem. Perhaps the child is caught in a loyalty bind, struggling, and thinking they would feel more comfortable with one parent.

Children want to love both parents and to enjoy their time with both. At some level, they may wish their parents still loved each other. Obviously, it would be easier on them if their parents could still be nice to each other; this would give them more peace and the feeling their family has a "normal" divorce.

If the parents intensely dislike each other, the child initially feels confused. They wonder, "Is Mom right that Dad is a jerk?" or, "What's going on with Dad that he put Mom in a situation where she feels so bad?" If the relationship distress between the child's parents continues for a long time, the child may end up taking sides with one parent. This alignment with one parent can relieve the child's confusion and ambivalent feelings. One parent is right; the other is wrong. One parent is lovable; the other is not. They want to spend all their time with one parent and none with the other.

When a child begins to express their preference not to follow the schedule of the parenting plan, the Neutral Coparent does several things. First, they express their understanding of the child's distress. Perhaps they say, "Oh honey, not getting along with someone you have deep feelings for can be so tough." Next, they suggest to the child ways the child might talk with the coparent. For example, if the coparent is teasing the child about their preference to eat only vegan foods, the Neutral Coparent could suggest, "The next time your dad makes a comment about how hard it is to keep food in the house for you, say to him, 'Dad, that makes me feel like you don't respect me, that me wanting to eating vegan is just a kid thing." The Neutral Coparent assures the child their dad wants to get along with them and will hear what they are saying, even if it takes the child having to repeat the message a few times. Or, the Neutral Coparent offers to talk with Dad in the child's presence in order to have a more in-depth conversation about what is happening, and discuss who needs to do what to short-circuit the growing parent-child tension. Above all, the Neutral Coparent is clear with the child that cutting off the relationship with the resisted parent is not an option. Not working through a problem or not following a court order are also not options. The Neutral Coparent's message is something like this: "All of your important relationships will involve ups and downs and having to work your way through tough feelings. I know that talking about relationship problems makes for difficult conversations that you want to avoid. But your relationship with your mother, just like your relationship with me, is precious; it must be protected."

After my child stopped going to their other parent's home, their stomach aches and headaches went away, and they started doing better at school and seemed happier. I want my child to have a relationship with their other parent, but not if it is harming my child. What should I do?

Parents often report that when a child does not have contact with a resisted parent, the child is less stressed and better adjusted. They observe the child performing better in school, moping around the house less, and talking about how much happier they feel. These observations can be a powerful incentive for the favored parent to resist a reunification intervention, and for the child to amplify and exaggerate their complaints about the resisted parent.

It is reasonable for the favored parent to worry that beginning or restarting the reunification process with the resisted parent will increase the stress level of the child, at least initially. But it is hard to know if this will happen, and it depends on several things.

In general, the longer the child has been allowed to avoid contact with the resisted parent, the more likely the child will feel stressed when the reunification process begins and contact with the resisted parent resumes. Allowing avoidance as a coping strategy for a challenging situation, rather than facing it, does not build resilience in children. Also, the child may have developed an attitude of empowerment—that is, they should be able to decide if they want a relationship with their resisted parent, and they should be able to decide to participate in therapy or not. If the child complains they are being coerced by the court to have a relationship they don't want, or to attend therapy they don't want, they may feel more stressed and become more oppositional.

The Escalated Coparent says to the child something like, "The court says you have to, and if you don't, I will get in trouble." Or, "You have to go to the intervention, but I will talk to my attorney about the fact that you really don't want to go." Or, "At your age you should be able to decide. I'll tell the judge that you think you should have a voice."

The Neutral Coparent says, "It's time. I've talked with your mom, and we agreed now is the time to bury the hatchet, and for all of us to find a way to get along better. We can figure this out. It will be slow going at first, but let's see what we can do to heal the family."

If the favored parent puts the full weight of their persuasive ability into clarifying for the child the importance of reconciling with the resisted parent, the stress on the child will likely be tolerable. Here is a rather dramatic example of how that can work. During an intervention, an 11-year-old girl ran into the bathroom at the psychologist's office and refused to come out when she was told that she would have to meet with Dad's new partner. The parents couldn't coax her out. The psychologist couldn't coax her out. Only when the parents and the new partner left the office was she willing to emerge. She was given some time to settle, and the intervention started up again. However, as soon as the new partner's name was mentioned, she again ran into the bathroom and would not come out. The psychologist told the parents that it seemed best to end the intervention, and she would meet with them the following Monday to figure out the next step. Over the weekend Mom emailed the psychologist that a meeting on Monday was not necessary. After Mom and daughter got home, Mom had a long talk with her. Several things had been said during the intervention that the daughter did not understand, and Mom explained that it was critical that the daughter give Dad's new partner a chance. The day after that talk, she and the child met with Dad and his new partner at a butterfly farm and had a nice afternoon. Mom, Dad, and his new partner assured the daughter that they understood her feelings and would work together to make sure she was doing okay when she was at Mom's house and at the new partner's house. Over time, the family worked through this issue, although it was difficult and slow going.

32 My child says they are too afraid to sleep at their other parent's home. How do I respond?

If a child says they are afraid to sleep at their other home, it is reasonable for any parent to ask their child what they are afraid of. It's also reasonable to ask a few other questions such as if they talked with the other parent about their fears, or if they are allowed to keep a light on. The Escalated Coparent interprets the child's problem as evidence of the coparent's poor parenting skills. They become convinced that the child is at risk of harm. They jump to conclusions. They may ask the child leading questions such as, "Why don't you feel safe at your daddy's house?" "Is everything okay over there between you and Daddy?" "What happens at Daddy's house that makes you afraid to sleep there?"

To comfort the child, the Escalated Coparent may secretly give a piece of their own clothing to the child to take with them, spray some of their daily perfume on the child's PJ's or allow them to sleep in their bed for comfort. If the child texts them after the child's bedtime, the Escalated Coparent exchanges multiple rounds of text messages with the child. The Escalated Coparent may object to the resisted parent taking the child's phone at bedtime, arguing the child needs it to feel secure. The Escalated Coparent insists the child be allowed to call them at bedtime. The Escalated Coparent tells the child their other parent should not have their bedroom door closed at night. Or worse, the Escalated Coparent assumes the child's problem with self-soothing is a basis for objecting to the child's having overnights at the other parent's home.

A Neutral Coparent asks the child questions such as, "What could help you feel more comfortable at Dad's house at night?" and then arranges to talk with the other parent to clarify what may be going on. A Neutral Coparent is willing to discuss that some of the child's sleeping arrangements at each home may need to be consistent and coordinated. For example, when the child awakens at night, if the favored parent allows the child to come into their room and crawl into bed with them, the parents may need to agree that after the child is comforted, the child must return to their own bed. Neutral Coparents talk together about how each of them gets the child ready for bed, what seems to work, and what the child does when they are manipulating to get more attention or to delay "lights out." Perhaps a short contact with the favored parent at bedtime is an agreed-upon strategy for a period of time to reassure the child. Most importantly, the coparents may agree to weekly reports about how the child slept while at their house.

In a highly diplomatic manner and knowing they have only part of the picture, a Neutral Coparent shares the child's concerns about why the resisted parent's home does not feel comfortable to the child. The Neutral Coparent knows that the child not feeling comfortable is not the same as the child not being safe. The Neutral Coparent keeps in mind that they don't truly know what is going on at the coparent's home, and that their child's reports may contain important omissions or exaggerations, or may be taken out of context. The Neutral Coparent knows that much like a snowball rolling downhill, when their child says they are afraid at night, the child's reported fears tend to fuel the coparent's thoughts and anxiety toward disaster scenarios that only serve to increase the child's anxiety.

My child says they don't want their other parent to attend their medical appointments. How can I handle this situation?

An Escalated Coparent may give late notice about the time of the appointments. In the waiting room, they may sit with the child away from the resisted parent and not acknowledge their presence. An Escalated Parent may refuse to be in the examining room with the child and resisted parent unless a medical professional is present. After the nurse has completed the preliminary examination, the Escalated Coparent may leave the room with the nurse in a dramatic statement of their dislike and distrust of the resisted parent.

A Neutral Coparent appreciates that tension between the coparents spills over and stresses the child. They understand that a child may say that they don't want the resisted parent to come to the appointment merely to avoid the parents fighting. A Neutral Coparent understands that participating in a child's health care is a fundamental parenting activity, and is a good place to bring the child in contact with the resisted parent. They make plans with the coparent to minimize stress on the child. For example, Neutral Coparents agree that they will exchange courteous greetings in the waiting area and that the child will be encouraged to connect with the other parent. They agree that both parents will initially meet with the medical professional without the child to provide background information regarding the presenting complaint. They ask that after the child has been examined, the child be given a summary of findings. Then the parents together will talk to the examining professional to receive a more detailed summary of findings and treatment recommendations.

PART THREE: COPARENTING TOOLS AND STRATEGIES

"If you always do what you've always done, you'll always get what you've always got."

–Henry Ford

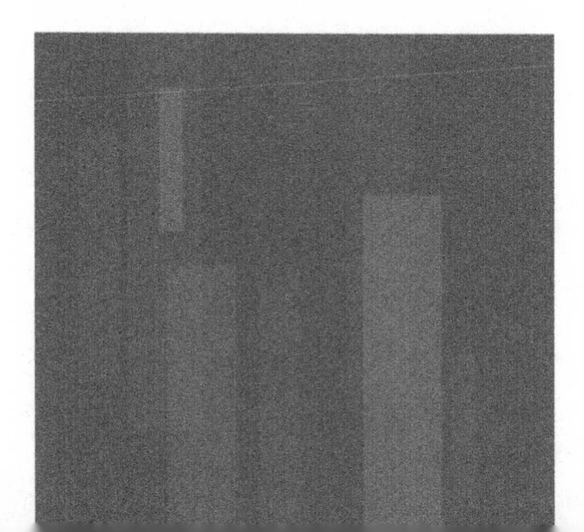

CHAPTER 14

Parallel Coparenting to De-escalate Conflict

PARALLEL COPARENTING TO DE-ESCALATE CONFLICT

When parents communicate with each other in families with RRP, the tension in the air is thick. The risk of conflict escalation is high. Coparents are often angry and do not trust each other. They doubt that effective coparenting communication and cooperation is possible. They fear that what they say may be used against them in court. They may worry the interventionist wants them to bury the hatchet and become friendly with each other. A practical model for coparents with intractable conflict is *parallel coparenting*.

In this model, parents disengage from interacting with each other as much as they can, while still adequately executing the shared responsibilities of parenting. With parallel coparenting, the parents more or less operate in parallel universes that the child travels between. Parallel coparenting minimizes opportunities for conflict. The parents de-escalate family conflict by minimizing engagement with each other and carefully following the specific requirements of the parenting plan.

The term "parallel coparenting" is somewhat unfortunate in that the child does not *live* in parallel universes. They have one family restructured into two home bases—they have one family life across two homes. Parents following a parallel coparenting plan must share child-focused information and make major decisions about the child living in two homes.

The following parallel coparenting guidelines (courtesy of Barbara Fidler, PhD) help parents to cooperate to raise the child and minimize coparenting conflict.

The Framework for Parallel Coparenting:

- Parents disengage and have little or no direct interactions with each other.
- Parents work independently for the best interests of their child.

- Nothing is assumed; everything is spelled out in the parenting plan.
- Each parent's household functions independently; each parent is responsible for making decisions about the child during the time the child is in that parent's household.
- In order to minimize conflict, there is no assumption of flexibility in scheduling.
- A parenting coordinator may be necessary to arbitrate parenting issues that are not specified by the parenting plan.

How Parallel Coparenting Works:

Scheduling Guidelines:

- The schedule is written down in detail and placed on a shared online calendar.[35]
- *Nothing* is left open to interpretation, because *loopholes breed conflict.*
- To minimize parental conflict and parental face-to-face contact, parenting time exchanges take place at neutral locations, such as school, daycare, or extracurricular activities.

Coparenting Communication Guidelines:

- Communication is polite and businesslike, but not personal.
- A wall exists between your parenting relationship and the rest of your personal life; nothing personal is shared with the other parent.
- *Neither parent is permitted to tell the other parent how to parent!*
- In the event of emergencies, parents' telephonic communication may be necessary. For example, a parent taking a child to an urgent care facility for emergency medical care will inform the other parent of the child's condition and the location of treatment as soon as possible.

- When parents do need to share information with each other in non-emergency matters, parents use email, text, fax (if there is privacy where the fax is received), a parenting notebook, or a pre-appointed third party (**never** the child). *Parents will avoid face-to-face communication whenever possible to avoid the risk of conflict escalation.*
- As much as possible, each parent bears the responsibility for obtaining information about the child. For example, each parent is responsible for contacting the school for notice of meetings, report cards, etc.

When Parents Need to Meet to Address an Issue Too Complex for Emails:

- Meetings are formal, held in a public place and scheduled by appointment at a mutually convenient time.
- Meetings and calls should take place during regular working hours and last no more than 30 minutes.
- Following meetings or communication, the parent initiating should send a summary of understandings and agreements reached. The other parent should send a response that confirms shared understandings and agreements, and identifies any details that require further clarification.
- Meetings may require the presence of a neutral third party.
- If any deviation or change from the agreed-upon plan or order is requested, negotiations will take place with the assistance of an agreed-upon neutral third party.

After separation and divorce, the coparenting relationship is often referred to as a "business relationship," meaning the coparents don't share personal information and they remain respectful. Rather, they stick to the business of raising the kids and any coparenting matters that require their mutual efforts. It can be hard for coparents to set the boundaries of what can and cannot be said to one another, especially immediately following the separation. Parents' communication following separation and divorce is the opposite of what happened at the beginning of the relationship. When the parents first met, they had essentially no information about each other. As the relationship deepened, communication flowed, more and more personal information was shared, and eventually they knew each other's deepest personal secrets and most embarrassing moments. When the intimate relationship ends, the cycle reverses. Parents no longer talk in-depth about their physical health, friendships, finances, and personal relationships. No longer are they entitled to criticize each other's behavior. For many coparents, this last boundary can be particularly difficult to establish and hold. Our case files are filled with emails between coparents containing threatening, hostile, belittling, sarcastic, and sometimes even vulgar statements and allegations.

In many states, parenting coordinator services are available for coparents who cannot negotiate coparenting issues without unreasonable amounts of conflict. A Parenting Coordinator is a behavioral health professional or an attorney who is appointed by the court or by parent agreement to assist the coparents to execute the court-ordered parenting plan. The Parenting Coordinator becomes the link between parents who are implementing a parallel parenting model. Parenting Coordinators meet with the parents to resolve disputes over issues, such as making minor adjustments to the parenting time schedule, setting the locations of parenting time exchanges, organizing the child's communication with the non-custodial parent, monitoring school-related problems, ensuring the timely exchange of medical information, and so forth. The role and authority of Parenting Coordinators varies considerably from state to state. Additional information about Parenting Coordinators is available online at: https://www.afccnet.org/Resource-Center/Resources-for-Families.

CHAPTER 14: KEY POINTS

- Parallel coparenting minimizes opportunities for conflict. The parents de-escalate family conflict by minimizing engagement with each other and carefully following the specific requirements of the parenting plan.
- Parents following a parallel coparenting plan must share child-focused information and make major decisions about the child living in two homes.
- After separation and divorce, the coparenting relationship is often referred to as a "business relationship," meaning the coparents don't share personal information and they remain respectful. Rather, they stick to the business of raising the kids and any coparenting matters that require their mutual efforts.

CHAPTER 15

Five Shifts to Becoming a Neutral Coparent

FIVE SHIFTS TO BECOMING A NEUTRAL COPARENT

> "The shift from escalation to de-escalation is not a single event, but rather a process that advances in a broad step-by-step fashion and is produced by pressures that build over time. This process includes trying to get adversaries to the negotiating table, forming agreements about peripheral issues, and moving toward resolution of the basic issues. All of this is typically accompanied by a reduction in hostility and mistrust between the adversaries."
>
> **–Michelle Maiese**[36]

When coparenting conflict is not resolved, it escalates and ensnares the children and the family network. As we have seen, escalated conflict can become intractable, permanently change family relationships, and negatively impact the health and adjustment of children and their parents.

The path most likely to bring a satisfactory outcome for RRP is compliance with the court-ordered parenting plan put into action through parallel parenting. This outcome may not allow for flexibility in the parenting time schedule, or for sharing more than essential information about the child's specific experience in each parent's home. However, parallel coparenting and compliance with the court-ordered parenting plan will minimize the engagement of coparents and decrease conflict. The child may be in a family in which the atmosphere is sometimes thick with residual hurt and resentment, but they will be protected from the toxic effects of intractable family conflict. And by remaining disengaged for a time while following coparenting agreements, it is possible that trust can build and parents may become more cooperative and conciliatory over time.

But even when the parents implement the court's plan through parallel coparenting, conflict often continues. Even minimal sharing of necessary information about the children as they transition back and forth between homes—the nuts and bolts of shared parenting—invariably results in conflict flare-ups.

In this chapter, we present five family shifts that can help coparents to be more neutral in their approach to one another.

Shift 1: Avoiding Conversation Triggers

> "All happy families resemble one another; each unhappy family is unhappy in its own way."
>
> **–Leo Tolstoy**

Effective coparents contain their conflict escalation to a narrow range. While talking about their differences, they stay calm and child-focused; they treat each other with respect. They listen carefully and try to understand each other's interests and worries. They discuss possible approaches to solving a problem together, and they select the most promising (or least undesirable) alternative. In contrast, when coparents allow conflict to escalate, a seemingly endless variety of conflict-provoking behaviors occur as they attempt to address child-related issues. In other words, conflict breeds more conflict. Conflict preys on vulnerabilities within the family. It reduces the family's ability to resolve and contain conflict.

Consider the following conflict triggers:[37]

Verbal Behaviors	Voice Tone	Gestures
Giving advice	Cold	Pointing a finger
Criticizing	Harsh	Crossed arms
Blaming	Loud	Shaking a fist
Complaining	Whining	Obscene gesture
Assuming	Flat	Turning away
Dismissing	Snickering	Rolling eyes
Being sarcastic	Groaning	Shaking head
Accusing	Sighing	Shrugging
Taking guilt trips	Issuing ultimatums	Interrupting

Amy Armstrong, LISW, refers often to the barriers of communication from her Real-Time Parenting Curriculum.[38] Although these habitual responses may be well intended, they are communication roadblocks that can actually increase hostility:

- Lecturing, preaching
- Inappropriately reassuring, sympathizing
- Diverting, withdrawing, distracting
- Questioning, probing, interrogating
- Praising, buttering-up
- Advising, giving solutions
- Interpreting, analyzing

The first few seconds following presentation of a conflict trigger are critical. As the well-known psychiatrist Viktor Frankl, MD, observed, "Between stimulus and response there is a space. In that space is our power to choose our response. In our response lies our growth and our freedom." Lois Gold, MSW, describes responses to conflict triggers that further escalate the conflict:[39]

- Immediately getting on the defensive
- Globalizations, e.g., "I am always accommodating to you."
- Cross-complaints
- Put-downs
- Should statements
- Lecturing
- Either/or statements
- Seeing issues from only your side
- Believing your interpretation is the correct interpretation
- Tending to interpret events negatively

- You can't or don't remember anything good from the past
- Tending to see the losses and suffering only in your own situation, and not in your coparent's. (You see your coparent as having the better deal rather than as someone with a different set of losses and problems.)
- Predicting the future based on the past, not recognizing that you are in the middle of a transition during which everything is undergoing change

Our analysis of the stages of intractable RRP discussed in Chapter 7 identifies these additional triggers:

- Arguments over truth and blame
- Polarized thinking that includes:
  1. Negative stereotypes of family members
  2. Open-and-shut conclusions
  3. Negative confirmation bias
  4. Unforgiving mindset springing from deep resentment

Coparents subjected to repeated episodes of intractable conflict become intensely sensitive to conflict triggers. Slight provocations cascade into coparents talking over each other, arguing about the details of what happened in the past, and jumping from incident to incident and topic to topic. The pace of conversation accelerates, emotional intensity increases, physiology moves to fight-flight-freeze mode, and the quality of critical thinking goes down.

Coparents are aware of most of these conflict triggers, so why do they keep falling victim to them? It's probably a combination of things:

1. They don't adequately appreciate the destructive impact they are having on their child.

2. They cannot resist reacting to the polarized thoughts and resentment caused by intractable family conflict.
3. They have personality vulnerabilities that existed prior to their relationship with their coparent that are intensified by the conflict.
4. Repeated exposure to RRP conflict changes the structure of a family member's brain architecture making them hyper-reactive to more RRP conflict.

Joseph LeDoux is a neuroscientist who studies how the brain detects and responds to threat. He identified that the amygdala in the brain receives input from the five senses without going through the prefrontal cortex where problem-solving and decision-making occur. Therefore, humans can experience intense emotional reactions, even panic attacks for no apparent reason, or "out of the blue." When a person feels threatened, the strength of neural activation from the amygdala can interfere with thinking and problem-solving. Daniel Goleman, PhD, in his popular book *Emotional Intelligence*, refers to the amygdala (brain) overriding thinking and problem-solving (mind) as "Emotional Hijacking." Emotional hijacking interferes with critical thinking—angry people are notorious for saying things they later regret.

Fearful fliers offer an example of emotional hijacking. Education about the safety statistics of flying does not help them overcome their fear. The anxiety that originates in a fearful flyer's amygdala convinces them that the flight they are on is the one-in-a-million that will crash. In families with parent-child contact problems, the resisted parent cannot provide enough evidence that the children are safe and secure while in their care, and the favored parent cannot provide enough evidence they are not undermining the children's relationship with the resisted parent.

In sum, the intractable conflict involves a complex system of conflict triggers that are tied to revolving multiple issues. Over time, coparents become more easily triggered and less able to manage conflict escalation. Thus, the first critical shift for de-escalating family conflict is to master the ability to STOP—to withdraw from conflict when it starts to escalate.

The general formula for disengaging is simple on paper: Follow the guidelines of parallel coparenting to minimize opportunities for conflict. When interacting, recognize early when the pressure of aggressive emotion is building. When a parent feels their emotional composure is slipping, they ask for a redirection or interruption of the conversation away from whatever is agitating them and their emotions, and they commit to resume their interaction within a specific timeframe. After their composure is restored, they resume the problem-solving discussion. Easier said than done.

Parents are pretty good at recognizing when angry aggression is building in their coparent, but are less quick to recognize it in themselves. For example, if a man has an anger management problem that could result in domestic violence, behavioral health professionals know to ask his partner how angry he is; she will have a more accurate reading than he will. He will say he is being passionate or speaking his truth. She will say he is escalating and getting closer to losing it.

Similarly, parents will be quicker to recognize their coparent's anger escalation than their own. Unfortunately, recognizing the coparent is escalating often does not always result in disengagement. In the face of an inaccurate or accusatory statement, the coparent may feel an overwhelming urge to set the record straight, leading to more engagement rather than less. As one parent said, "I know it's my responsibility to stop the arguments, but I felt it was so important for him to understand what I was trying to say that I kept going."

A lot of information is available online and in self-help books about how to defuse arguments. But coparents with parent-child contact problems are not trying to defuse an argument. Their conflict is many times more severe than a normal range argument. They are trying to end a holy war waged to defend the child against what they view as mortal (and moral) threats to the child's growth, development and well-being. Rather than defusing, the first step needs to be a cease-fire.

Either one parent acting alone, or the parents acting together, must disengage and resist the urge to counter-argue the next inaccurate or attacking statement.

Here is a list of escalation-stopping statements:

- "Do we need to agree about this?"
- "I'm noticing my chest is tightening up. I'm afraid I might say something to make things worse, so I'm feeling reluctant to speak."[40]
- "I notice I'm wanting to strike out at you verbally right now, and I'm telling you this so that I'll be less likely to act it out."
- "Look, we're not about to change each other's minds about this right now, but I wouldn't mind talking it over with you later."[41]
- "Look, I don't want to discuss this anymore. Maybe we can talk about it another time when we've both calmed down. I know the issue needs to be resolved soon, so I'll send an email about my availability in the next couple days."
- "I understand you are saying something that may be important for me to understand, but I need to stop the conversation and catch my breath at this point. Later, I can get more clarity about your concern, and we can discuss what I do and don't agree with about what you are saying."

Notice the "I" statements in the list above. The speaker takes responsibility for their own feelings, rather than saying something like, "You are being such a jerk! There's no point in trying to talk when you are acting like this." Notice too that the speaker is not caving in; they are clear there is something they need to say, but now is not the right time.

When the speaker asks for a conversational stop, it needs to be honored. However, when things are calmer, they should take the responsibility to schedule a time to talk again about the issue at hand.

On the other hand, when coparents trust they will stop escalation when one of them asks for a time-out, they begin to think they can trust each other to have a civil conversation.

Shift 2: Manage the Conversation

In families with RRP, coparents dread talking with each other for good reason. Even simple encounters can ignite brain-flame. Here are some tips for managing conversations between polarized family members:

- Structure the conversation to resemble a formal business meeting.
- Set an appointment to talk at a time when distractions and stress are minimized for you and your coparent. An appointment should include start time, duration, and place (neutral, free of distraction). A phone appointment may support your interaction better than a face-to-face meeting.
- Develop an agenda and a list of issues to be talked about, and share this ahead of time so that both of you are prepared. When an issue not on the list is introduced, it probably is best to postpone talking about it until another time. Surprises are rarely conducive to a constructive discussion.
- Create an agenda. Prioritize the issues to be talked about. Start with simpler problems that have fewer triggers.
- Take turns talking about issues and share the total time equitably so that both of you get time for your concerns.
- While talking about a selected issue, keep in mind the procedure that has been developed as a general negotiation principle: The person with the issue presents their concern; the other person responds; then each person gets a turn to offer a rebuttal statement. Following this procedure gives each person two chances to express their thoughts, and after four presentations the major points should be clear.

- Focus on one specific issue at a time; do not let the conversation jump from topic to topic.
- Focus on the problem, not the person. Keep talking about the homework conditions at the other parent's home, rather than "the things you allow at your house." When conflict escalates, the conversation goes from talking about the who, what, where, when, and why of what happened, to generalizations about character (such as, "You always..." and "You never..."), and, too often, stereotypes (such as, "You are a narcissist…" or "You have borderline personality disorder").
- Learn to state your concern in a single sentence. This takes practice and skill. You may feel what you have to say is morally right, and you have a right to say it, but the more drawn out your concerns are, the more likely conflict escalation becomes. If you find yourself going on for more than four or five sentences, recover by saying something like, "Here is my main point..." If your coparent is rattling on, politely say something like, "I'm getting lost in the details. What is your main point?"

Conversation Practice: To prepare for communicating with your coparent, write down a list of "headlines" you would like to bring up. Start the conversation by saying something like, "Here are the main points I want you to consider today." Then, if the conversation becomes bogged down in details, you could say something like, "I think we are getting into too many details. Can we think of proposals to address my main points?"

Shift 3: Asking to Listen

In college, one of the authors learned to use "The Magic Sword," an approach to conflict de-escalation that became his go-to response for many stressful encounters. The Magic Sword is to go "one down" to an angry person, rather than trying to be "one up" and show them that their arguments are somehow wrong. Going one down means responding to another's angry statements by saying something like, "I want to be sure I understand what you are saying. Please say it again in a somewhat different way so I can be sure that I get it." Or, "I think I get what you are saying, but let me ask some questions to be sure." Or, "Can you give me an example to help me see it more clearly?"

Asking to listen communicates that what the coparent is saying deserves the respect to be heard and thought about. Intractable conflict involves massive attacks on each parent's self-esteem. When a coparent hears that what they are trying to communicate is being listened to respectfully, their anger can quickly reduce.

Asking to listen is different from *Active Listening,* a popular approach to conflict resolution. Active Listening[42] involves paying attention, withholding judgment, reflecting, clarifying, summarizing, and sharing. For coparents with intractable conflict, Active Listening may be too ambitious a goal. The potential for conflict escalation is too high. If a parent tries to convey sympathy when the coparent or child is still angry, negative confirmation bias may kick in, and the coparent or child will think to themselves something like, "Right, you are trying to butter me up because you want something."

Shift 4: From Problems to Proposals

Clearly, coparents with parent-child contact problems have a lot of issues needing solutions. As interventionists, we hear many accounts of how the problems began, how they worsened and how efforts to solve them have been outrageously expensive and ineffective. Parents tend to "go into the weeds" talking about a problem's negative elements. The more they talk and think about the negative evidence, the more likely they are to conclude the problem is hopeless.

Mediator, attorney, and therapist Bill Eddy, LCSW, Esq., pointed out that when people focus on proposals rather than problems, the conversation shifts from the past to the future. The focus shifts from blaming each other to taking responsibility and finding solutions to problems.[43] We could not agree more. When family members focus on what they can do differently *going forward*, a major shift toward de-escalation occurs. However, it is hard to keep the conversation focused on solutions and proposals. Thoughts about the past invariably crop up, and if these are expressed, the tiger is out of the cage. Families with moderate to severe RRP cannot seem to keep the conversation focused on solutions, despite their best intentions and efforts. They need a third party to manage the conversation.

Here is an example of a problem-solving conversation that begins problem-focused and then becomes solution-focused:

Mother: The kids aren't getting their schoolwork done at your house.

Father: Yes, they are. I sit with them and make sure they do.

Mother: Look at Jamaya's last four math tests.
She did poorly on the ones that happened after your parenting time.

Father: I went over those problem sets with her. She knew them. I don't know what happened.

Mother: Well, Jamaya tells me you get mad at her if she doesn't do them right and you tell her how to do them.

Father: Not true. You don't know what goes on at my house. I am so sick of you telling me how to parent.

Mother: Jamaya tells me she tries to do her homework at school or in her room so she doesn't have to be around you.

Father: Let it alone! Both kids sit with me at the table after dinner, and it's a pretty good time for us.

Mother: You don't know what it's really like for those kids.

Father: If you didn't give them the third-degree when they come back to your house, they wouldn't have to complain about my house to make you feel okay.

Mother: Okay. How about if I focus on math problem sets with Jamaya, and you focus on reading with Will?

Father: But how will that help with the math tests?

Mother: I'll work ahead with her on the assignments. Her teacher told me she would be happy to let me know what these are gonna be.

Father: Okay. And I'll be responsible for Will's next book review project.

Mother: Sounds good, agreed.

Shift 5: From Fixed Mindsets to Growth Mindsets

As we have discussed, stereotypes about the offending parent imply they have not changed and are incapable of change. A characteristic of people with interpersonal challenging personalities is that they are inefficient in learning from their mistakes. However, it seems absurd to think that family members do not learn and change in response to the extraordinary difficulty of RRP.

Carol S. Dweck, PhD, a psychology professor from Stanford University, teaches about important differences in approaching challenges with a "fixed" versus a "growth" mindset. The *fixed* mindset assumes that a person has a fixed amount of a personal quality, for example, intelligence. Under that assumption, when a person has trouble learning an academic subject, it is because they just aren't smart enough. A *growth* mindset assumes that intelligence can be grown, that the thing being learned can be acquired with enough effort, and so people should work harder when facing difficulties because their effort will be rewarded with learning.[44] Dweck acknowledges: "(1) we're all a mixture of fixed and growth mindsets, (2) we will probably always be, and (3) if we want to move closer to a growth mindset in our thoughts and practices, we need to stay in touch with our fixed-mindset thoughts."[45]

It is not easy to hold a growth mindset about intractable RRP—to believe that everyone is learning healthy lessons from the difficult family struggles. Rather, even when a parent recognizes the value of staying in a growth mindset, the thoughts generated in their mind will include fixed mindset thoughts, such as Dad has not changed one bit; or Mom only wants the kids for herself. Dweck offers sage advice for parents and children when she says, "We need to stay in touch with our fixed-mindset thoughts." A TED talk of Dr. Dweck is available at: https://www.ted.com/talks/carol_dweck_the_power_of_believing_that_you_can_improve?language=en.

CHAPTER 15: KEY POINTS

- The path most likely to bring a satisfactory outcome for RRP is compliance with the court-ordered parenting plan put into action through parallel parenting.
- Effective coparents contain their conflict escalation to a narrow range.
- The first critical shift for de-escalating family conflict is to master the ability to STOP—to withdraw from conflict when it starts to escalate.
- Parents are pretty good at recognizing when angry aggression is building in their coparent, but less quick to recognize it in themselves.
- When coparents trust they will stop escalation when one of them asks for a time-out, they begin to think they can trust each other to have a civil conversation.
- Intractable conflict involves massive attacks on each parent's self-esteem. When a coparent hears that what they are trying to communicate is being respectfully listened to, their anger can quickly reduce.
- When family members focus on what they can do differently going forward rather than who made mistakes in the past, a major shift toward de-escalation occurs.

CHAPTER 16

From Resentment to Reconnection

FROM RESENTMENT TO RECONNECTION

> "Guilt, regret, resentment, grievances, sadness, bitterness, and all forms of nonforgiveness are caused by too much past, and not enough presence."
>
> **–Eckhart Tolle**

In Chapter 8, resentment was defined as a lasting feeling of ill will caused by an act regarded as unjust, wrong, insulting, or hurtful. We pointed out that resentments generate a fixed, unforgiving mindset in family members. They become reluctant to admit one's own mistakes, and experience a lack of compassion for the suffering of other family members. Often, they find themselves with vengeful wishes and thoughts.

The powerful impact of resentment is reflected in a statement by a dad who had justified anger toward his coparent—she had abducted his daughter out of the country, and he had not seen his daughter in several years. The dad said, "A week before I saw my daughter, I had made a prayer that I would let go of any hatred and malice in my heart if I could get my daughter back. But when I saw her mother that first time in court, a rage like no other was in my soul. I have never had so much hatred for someone. It hurt me."

It is difficult to overcome resentment because it develops in response to feeling unjustly hurt. For example, a 15-year-old female was asked, "What are you doing to get rid of the resentment?" She responded, "Just kind of ignore it. I don't think that what I feel is helpful, but I don't think it is wrong either. I think it's well founded."

Offering apologies is a crucial step for reducing resentment by the other in a relationship.

Apologies

Apologies play an important role in every family with RRP. The coparents could apologize to each other for their part in allowing the conflict to escalate to destructive proportions. The parents could offer the children a joint apology for putting them through a hard divorce. The resisted parent may apologize to the child for allowing a strain to develop in their relationship and offer a series of apologies regarding specific grievances expressed by the child.

Children usually want an apology from the resisted parent and sometimes insist on one as a condition to work on the strained relationship. This condition should be viewed as encouraging since it means that the door to reconnection is still open. The apology the child desires is not necessarily to hear the parent say "I'm sorry"; often the child wants to hear the parent acknowledge that the child's grievances require in-depth discussion. The child may be saying "admit that you hurt me," as much as they are saying "admit that you did something wrong."

The first step toward making an apology is to understand what the child's hurt has been like, and to communicate authentic appreciation for the suffering the child has endured. This can be accomplished by asking the child to tell you about how hard it has been for them. And since children have limited vocabularies for expressing their feelings, the parents may need to ask questions to help them find words. Parents could ask something like the following:

- "Was the hurt so intense that you feel like it damaged you?"
- "Have you ever had feelings that strong before? Did they feel like they cut really deep into you and your heart?"
- "Were the feelings so strong there are no words to describe them?"
- "Did the hurt leave you with a feeling of bitter anger?"
- "Was the hurt so bad that you wished you could hurt me back?"

When a child says, "Nobody is listening to me," they may only be complaining that they are not getting their way. However, they may be pleading for a parent to understand the depth and extent of their hurt, anger, and sadness. The child may be trying to say, "This is so messed up and unfair."

It is not uncommon for the child to demand an apology for an act the resisted parent believes has been exaggerated, or that they did not do. During interventions, we teach all the family members about the unreliability of memory. That is, we point out that memories are not photographs or movies of what happened. Rather, memories are "constructed"; that is, we recall parts of an event, interpret what the event meant to us, and then tell and retell a story about what happened. We therapists are not trying to invalidate anyone's memory. We recognize that although a memory may not be entirely accurate, it is rarely fictitious. Laying a foundation about the unreliability of memory is intended to get the family out of a dead-end debate about whether the resisted parent is or is not a liar.

The resisted parent needs to take as much responsibility as they can for past bad behaviors, and talk about how they have learned from their mistakes. For example, a resisted parent might say, "I don't recall pushing you down the stairs, but I get it that you view me as someone who has a problem with anger. I totally agree with you about that. There have been lots of times that I got frustrated with you, and I responded with too much anger. I want to talk about each instance that you remember, especially if we focus on how I can do things better going forward. Without a doubt, I am guilty. I pray that you will forgive me."

The core elements of apologies include: 1) accepting responsibility, 2) promising better behavior in the future, and 3) making restitution.[46]

Accepting responsibility means avoiding excuses, arguments, and defensive justifications.

Pro tip: Be careful making "I" statements when offering an apology. The child may say, "Like always, your apology is about you. About how 'I'm sorry' and 'I wish I didn't do it' and 'I won't do it again'." In short, don't make the apology about *your* behavior. Make it about the suffering of the person you have hurt.

The resisted parent can count on the child making repeated accusations of bad parenting behavior. Offering facts to prove the accusation is inaccurate is not going to get anywhere, but a parent expressing self-responsibility in a credible way is hard to argue against. For example, a 10-year-old girl refused to see her mom. During the marriage, Mom had been subjected to domestic violence, and she acknowledged that she had made mistakes. Some weekends, she stayed in bed all day. She was irritable and depressed. She worked long hours to avoid being home, and when her daughter started to show an alliance with Dad, Mom accused her daughter of betraying her. Mom might take responsibility by saying something like, "You know your dad and I had hard times when we were together, and I got so upset I was lost. I lost my self-esteem. I lost my drive. I lost my temper. I lost my sense of who I was and the kind of mom I needed to be. I made a lot of mistakes and you got hurt, really hurt, and the court stuff between Dad and me since then has kept on hurting you. I am so disappointed in myself that I let all this happen. I pray that I have learned from the mistakes I made and that I am prepared to be a better parent to you now. Learning from my mistakes seems to be the only redemption I can earn."

That apology is a lot more than saying "I'm sorry." A key to its effectiveness is the parent talking about what was going on inside of themselves that led them to make poor choices. When an apology includes the parent's thoughts about personal internal dysfunction, the child is more likely to think that the parent means what they say.

Usually one apology is not enough to reduce the anger, distrust, and resentment to the point that more friendly behavior appears. The distrust that comes with RRP is profound.

Promising Better Behavior and Making Restitution

A parent's promise of better behavior sounds lame to a resentful child. They are a long way away from accepting a parent's promise to do better as a basis for trying to repair the relationship. Often the child says something to the parent like, "I've been through a lot of counseling about all of this. What have you done to become a better person?" If the resisted parent is able to offer only something like, "I talk to your stepmother about it, and she has helped me a lot," the parent will be arguing from a very weak position. The child wants to hear that the resisted parent has taken the steps they should have taken, given the suffering they have caused the child. That is, they have done something meaningful to make restitution. They have not only addressed the problem; they have taken extensive steps to correct it.

However, even when a parent has had a lot of counseling since the parent-child split, the child will be skeptical that meaningful change has occurred. Over time, real-time experience with the resisted parent may lead the child to change their polarized thinking and negative attitudes. But a parent can use the apology process to demonstrate they have changed their attitudes and are now capable of being a better parent.

We find that children want to focus for a long time on the wrongs they have suffered. They are receptive to a parent's message, "I want to understand everything about how hard this has been for you. Can you give me other examples?" They may talk about the same incident more than once but at different levels of meaning.

The child's airing of their grievance(s) provides the resisted parent a chance to demonstrate that they are handling things better. The parent listens, asks for clarification, and repeatedly takes responsibility. It can take a long time, but eventually the child may begin to trust that the parent's ability to hear and skillfully respond to the child's distress is reliable. It is as if the child realizes at some point, "Maybe he really does get it. Maybe he will be more careful next time."

From Resentment to Forgiveness

> "It is one of the greatest gifts you can give yourself, to forgive. Forgive everybody."
>
> **Maya Angelou**

Nancy Collier, LCSW, pointed out: "To let go of a grudge we need to move the focus off of the one who wronged us, off of the story of our suffering and into the felt experience of what we actually lived inside; our pain shifts from something that happened to us to a sensation that we know intimately, a felt sense that we know from the inside [...] We take responsibility for caring about our own suffering, and for knowing that our suffering matters, which can never be accomplished through the grudge, no matter how fiercely we believe in it."[47]

Here is the statement of an 18-year-old describing what it was like for him to develop forgiveness toward his father: "It was painful and emotional. I was trying to deal with my feelings of justified anger and unjustified hate. I did make some problems. He is not doing it to me anymore [the teen left for college]. Why should I hold that hate against him? There were many nights of crying over what he did, and nights of crying over how I need to stop crying over what he did. It was very emotional. It took a long time. It was most certainly a process. It took at least a year, at least a year. It was hard but I have forgiven him; I don't hold a grudge. The pain is there, the scars are there, but there is no more blood gushing out of it."

The young man shows that although he found forgiveness in his heart for his father, he did not feel obligated to allow his father to have the contact with him that he wanted. The forgiveness was for the young man, not his father.[48] When he says, "The pain is there, the scars are there, but there is no more blood gushing out of it," he shows that the anger is gone after he forgives, but hurt and sadness remain. Or, as another child said, "The pain is gone but the memories are still there."

It stands to reason that if the parents have not done their own forgiveness work, they will not be able to help the children with it.

To be clear, forgiveness is not about pardoning a transgression or saying, "No hard feelings." Forgiveness is going inside the self and looking for left-over anger and resentment, and then letting it go.

As resentment recedes, willingness to treat the other parent with respect emerges. The opposite can be true too: when parents and children treat one another with respect, resentment diminishes. Treating another family member with respect is something we all know how to do. But making yourself behave respectfully can be hard, especially when conflict starts to escalate. This is especially true for children. Children can be ruthless with the resisted parent. One would think that coparents would easily agree that their children should treat adults with respect. But until the favored parent reduces their own anger and resentment, they will not be effective in motivating the child to give the resisted parent their due respect. Conversely, if the resisted parent has reduced their anger and resentment, they will be able to talk to the child about the favored parent in a manner that demonstrates respect, and they will be able to respond to the child's disrespect toward them with compassion.

Fred Luskin, PhD, director of the Stanford/Northern Ireland Hope Project, said the following about forgiveness during a PBS interview:

> "There's a wonderful definition of forgiveness: that to forgive is to give up all hope for a better past [...] There's clear evidence that if people apologize, it's easier to forgive. Forgiveness, though, is not limited by that. You can forgive even if the person utters no conciliatory words and suffers no consequence, because forgiveness is always for

you. You forgive by remembering what happened and you commit yourself to it never happening again. Or, you can remember it and say, 'I'm not going to suffer any more. I'm going to bring some goodness to the people in my life.' It's an active quality. It has nothing to do with forgetting. And it's a very powerful statement."[49]

CHAPTER 16: KEY POINTS

- Offering apologies in a relationship is a crucial step for reducing the other's resentment.
- In asking for an apology, the child may be saying "admit that you hurt me," as much as they are saying "admit that you did something wrong."
- The core elements of apologies include: 1) accepting responsibility, 2) promising better behavior in the future, and 3) making restitution.
- Accepting responsibility means avoiding excuses, arguments, and defensive justifications.
- Forgiveness is not about pardoning a transgression or saying, "No hard feelings." Forgiveness is going inside the self and looking for left-over anger and resentment, and letting it go.

CHAPTER 17

What Makes Family Therapy More or Less Likely to Succeed

WHAT MAKES FAMILY THERAPY MORE OR LESS LIKELY TO SUCCEED

"A house divided against itself cannot stand."

–Abraham Lincoln

Social science has yet to accumulate enough high-quality research studies that data-based predictions can be offered to a family about the likely benefits of an RRP intervention.[50] However, research on the broad topic of conflict resolution and case studies about the results of RRP interventions clarify thinking about what makes family therapy more or less likely to succeed.

Research also does not provide a basis for estimating the likelihood that if the child is allowed a time-out from the resisted parent, the child will change their attitude and seek to restore contact. The consensus among our professional colleagues is that while this may occur, it is highly unusual with all but the mildest RRP cases.

A Perspective from the United Nations

You may recall in Chapter 6 we noted that our thinking about RRP has been informed by the work of international peace scholars. For example, The Family Conflict Curve presented in Chapter 6 is adapted from the work of Guy and Heidi Burgess of The Beyond Intractability Consortium at the University of Colorado.

The work of peace scholars at the United Nations presents another framework for thinking about intractable RRP conflict. The United Nations identifies a spectrum of activities related to peace and security that include:

- Prevention of conflict
- Peacemaking – addressing conflicts in progress and bringing hostile parties to a negotiated agreement

- Peacekeeping – coordinating actions among several parties to develop a basis for sustainable peace
- Peacebuilding – a long-term, comprehensive process of addressing core issues related to conflict [51]

We want to emphasize again the importance of the family de-escalating conflict as a necessary condition for resolving RRP. The family's initial efforts at peacemaking, that is, negotiating solutions to RRP, have not succeeded. Rather, the conflict escalated. Then a peacekeeping team (the court, parents, attorneys, and behavioral health professionals) needs to be put in place before peacemaking efforts can succeed. Peacebuilding, that is, addressing the core issues that led to RRP, is a long-term project. Coparents may never agree on what led to RRP. That is alright as long as they are able to agree that the child needs to have a healthy relationship with both parents. to be well adjusted in all the major areas of their lives (health, school, friends, relationships).

It is necessary, however, for both parents to respond to a core issue of RRP but in different ways. The resisted parent needs to respond to the child's historical grievances and demonstrate they can be a good parent. The favored parent needs to convince the child that it is time to reconnect with the resisted parent. Unless the favored parent provides adequate support, reduction of the strained parent-child relationship will occur at a snail's pace, if at all.

In sum, the United Nations framework describes steps that will make it more likely to resolve RRP.

A Perspective from The Stages of Change Model

The Stages of Change model, developed by Prochaska and DiClemente in the late 1970s, grew out of their work with smoking cessation—an intractable problem. The Stages of Change model holds that people move through six stages of change:

1. Precontemplation – People in this stage are unaware of their problem and are reluctant to talk about it.
2. Contemplation – People recognize their behavior may be problematic and are willing to think and talk about the pros and cons of changing their behavior.
3. Preparation – People start taking small steps toward changing their behavior, and acknowledge that change will be healthy.
4. Action – People have changed their behavior for an extended period, for example 60 days, and state their intention to continue to do so.
5. Maintenance – People have maintained change for a significant period of time, for example six months, and work to prevent relapse into earlier stages.
6. Termination – People have no desire to return to their unhealthy behaviors and are sure they will not relapse. This stage is rarely reached, as people tend to stay in the maintenance stage.

When an intervention starts, family members may be in the precontemplation stage. As the family builds confidence in the intervention, they become receptive to thinking about how their behavior may be problematic, and they take small steps toward change. If the family therapist successfully navigates the minefield of problems that can derail confidence in the intervention, the therapy may and must continue long enough that small steps are consolidated into lasting change.

Family members may have different degrees of readiness to change, both in general and on specific issues. For example, a resisted parent may be ready to stop blaming their coparent and reacting to conflict triggers. But they may not be ready to give up their role as an "authority" with the child, even though the child will barely talk to them let alone obey them. As another example, both parents may be ready for an all-family meeting to tell the child it is time to restart parenting time with the resisted parent, but the child stubbornly insists that they are entitled to dictate if, when, and how that will happen.

The bottom line is because parents love their children they want to resolve RRP. They typically get stuck at some stage of the change process. With skillful assistance from legal and behavioral health professionals, family members see what needs to be done, and take action steps resulting in lasting change.

What Makes Family Therapy Less Likely to Succeed

Well-regarded researchers such as Michael Saini, PhD; Barbara Fidler, PhD; and Nicholas Bala, JD, have studied coparenting conflict and the risk of intractable RRP developing. Within their various publications and presentations, they conclude that the risk for intractable RRP is greater and the prognosis less favorable if and when some of the following circumstances are present:[52]

- Multiple previous involvements with family court
- Repeated instances of non-compliance with court orders
- History of repeated intimate partner violence
- A coparent who insists on a custody/access evaluation to prove that their coparent is unfit
- History of resistance to or non-cooperation with RR family therapy
- A coparent with a diagnosed and untreated mental condition (psychotic disorder, substance abuse disorder, bipolar disorder, major depressive disorder)
- A parent's therapist diagnosed the presence of a personality disorder in their client
- Ongoing litigation regarding financial issues
- A substantial period of no contact between the resisted parent and the child

- Failure of previous RR family therapy interventions
- A coparent makes repeated allegations of child abuse that are unsubstantiated after child protection investigations
- Following multiple unsubstantiated allegations of child abuse, a coparent continues to allege that their coparent poses a genuine risk of significant harm to the child
- A new partner/spouse, grandparent, or other individual connected to the family who undermines a therapeutic intervention's effectiveness

What Makes Family Therapy More Likely to Succeed

RR family therapy interventions are more likely to succeed when some of the following circumstances are present:

- Coparents cooperated in raising the child before the onset of RRP.
- After the onset of RRP, coparents are sometimes able to communicate and negotiate solutions to issues.
- Coparents have a history of flexing the parenting time schedule to accommodate special events.
- The child had a good relationship with the resisted parent before onset of RRP.
- The child's resistance is in the mild to mild-moderate range, such as:
  - Mild Resistance: The child shows some resistance before transitions but quickly becomes comfortable with the other parent
  - Mild-to-Moderate Resistance: The child's family time with the resisted parent occurs, but it tends to be sporadic, infrequent, or delayed.
  - Severe Resistance: The child and the resisted parent have infrequent or no contact for a significant length of time.[53]

- The coparents seek an early intervention for RRP from a qualified professional.
- Parents seek advice from attorneys with reputations for mediating conflicts rather than litigating.
- Neither parent alleges severe domestic violence, child sexual abuse, or parental unfitness.

Coparenting Coordination and Cooperation: The Key to Your Child's Well-Being

> "Don't dwell on what went wrong. Instead, focus on what to do next. Spend your energy moving forward together toward an answer."
>
> **–Denis Waitley**

The ultimate goal of overcoming the alienation crisis is a good relationship between the resisting child and the resisted parent. Reaching that goal means overcoming the legacy of horrors that can accompany RRP. The heart of the healing process begins with the coparents re-establishing a functional coparenting relationship. Usually, before this can happen, a lot of preliminary work needs to be done to coordinate the efforts of the court, attorneys, and behavioral health professionals involved with the family. This work can be time consuming and expensive, but it is doable.

We find that once the stage is set, with the help of a well-trained behavioral health professional, coparents can communicate and reach agreements about the kinds of issues presented in the 33 Coparenting Solutions section of this book. The parents may not feel comfortable or have more than shallow trust in one another and the RR family therapy process, but their love for the child makes them persist.

A singular challenge to overcoming the alienation crisis is the negative pull of the Three Dementors. The impact of the intractable conflict on the family creates a "black hole" into which all signs of hope disappear.[54] Over time, the family gets hyper-sensitized to the conflict, and even small provocations trigger the collapse and disconnect response. In our experience, the family makes progress during a therapy session, then soon afterward they are back in very pessimistic mindsets. Sometimes the negativity re-asserts itself in response to an incident. Sometimes it resurfaces simply with the passage of time. It is critical that the coparents have frequent and easy access to the family therapist to talk about bumps in the road, and to work on their thought and emotional processes surrounding the RRP. Perhaps the hardest work family members must do to overcome the alienation crisis is working through their "demented" thoughts and feelings that develop in response to the horrific conflict of RRP.

In closing, we want to emphasize that the courts, legal, and behavioral health professionals are highly concerned about the devastating impact RRP can have. A lot of effort is going into educating professionals and developing innovative, evidence-based procedures for preventing and reducing the impact of RRP. The field is advancing, and progress is being made in providing parents the resources they need to support their efforts to protect their child.

Overcoming the alienation crisis requires overcoming the worst of hurts, the most persistent of angers, and the deepest of distrusts. It requires coordinating efforts with a coparent and professionals who at times seem suspect. It means staying at the negotiating table regardless of setbacks, and taking small steps until the sting of conflict is soothed by the balm of peacemaking. The path down the Family Conflict Curve is difficult, maybe even treacherous, but your desire to provide your child the best possible preparation for adulthood will propel you through all the challenges.

> "Peace is a daily, a weekly, a monthly
> process, gradually changing opinions,
> slowly eroding old barriers, quietly
> building new structures."
>
> **–John F. Kennedy**

CHAPTER 17: KEY POINTS

- The resisted parent needs to respond to the child's historical grievances and persuade the child that they can be a good parent. The favored parent needs to persuade the child that it is time to reconnect with the resisted parent.
- Family members may have different degrees of readiness to change both in general and on specific issues.
- The heart of the healing process begins with the coparents re-establishing a functional coparenting relationship.
- We find that with the help of a well-trained behavioral health professional, coparents can communicate and reach agreements.
- Perhaps the hardest work family members must do to overcome the alienation crisis is working through their "demented" thoughts and feelings that develop in response to the devastating conflict of RRP.

ABOUT THE AUTHORS

Drs. Moran, McCall, and Sullivan first worked together at Overcoming Barriers, Inc. family camps. Since then, they have collaborated on cases in the community and made presentations together at professional conferences. Dr. Moran, Dr. Sullivan, and Tyler Sullivan coauthored the earlier book *Overcoming the Coparenting Trap: Essential Parenting Skills When a Child Resists a Parent.*

John A. Moran, PhD, is a forensic clinical psychologist who has specialized in the field of high-conflict families for more than 35 years. He has published in peer-reviewed journals and books. He is an invited presenter at regional and national conferences on the topic of resist–refuse problems. He is on the Board of Directors of Overcoming Barriers, Inc. and has served as clinical director at OCB family camps. For more information his website is www.jamoranphd.com.

Shawn McCall, PsyD, Esq., is an attorney and psychologist who has been active in the San Francisco Bay Area psychological and legal communities. He has been involved in professional leadership roles and published in local publications. Dr. McCall has delivered presentations locally and nationally about parenting and coparenting in situations involving conflict, among other topics. He has provided clinical, forensic, and expert services to criminal, family, civil, and dependency courts in multiple states, and he has recently begun to practice law with a focus on family law. As part of Dr. McCall's commitment

About the Authors

to providing accessible services to all, he dedicates a portion of his practice to pro bono and reduced fee psychological and legal services.

Matthew J. Sullivan, PhD, has been in private practice in Palo Alto, California, specializing in forensic and clinical work in the Family Courts for 30 years. He is the author of numerous peer-reviewed articles, book chapters, and books on topics related to work in high-conflict shared-custody situations. He is an international pioneer in the development of the Parenting Coordination role.

He is the 2019–2020 President of the Association of Family and Conciliation Courts (AFCC) international organization. He served on the American Psychological Association Ethics Committee from 2016–2018. He is the cofounder of Overcoming Barriers, Inc., which is a nonprofit organization that has developed a variety of innovative programs for high-conflict shared-custody arrangements. For more information his website is www.sullydoc.com.

NOTES

Chapter 1

1. Leslie Drozd and Marsha Kline-Pruett, "Not Just Alienation: Resistance, Rejection, Reintegration, and Realities of Troubled Parent-Child Relationships," Association of Family and Conciliation Courts, Webinar, May 7, 2019. https://www.afccnet.org/Member-Center/Webinar-Archives/ctl/ViewConference/ConferenceID/282/mid/776.
2. Richard Gardner, "Recent Trends in Divorce and Custody Litigation," *The Academy Forum*, 29(2)(1985): 3–7.
3. Janet Johnston and Matthew Sullivan, "Parental Alienation: In Search of Common Ground for a More Differentiated Theory," *Family Court Review*, (2020), in press.
4. Barbara Fidler, Nicholas Bala, and Michael Saini, *Children Who Resist Post-Separation Parental Contact: A Differential Approach for Legal and Mental Health Professionals* (New York, NY: Oxford University Press, 2012).
5. Michael Saini, Leslie Drozd, and Nancy Olesen, "Adaptive and Maladaptive Gatekeeping Attitudes and Behaviors: Implications for Child Outcomes Following Separation and Divorce." *Family Court Review*, 55 (2017): 260–272. doi:10.1111/fcre.12276
6. Joan Kelly and Janet Johnston, "The Alienated Child: A Reformulation of Parental Alienation Syndrome," *Family Court Review*, 39, (2001): 249–266.
7. Richard Warshak, "Bringing Sense to Parental Alienation: A Look at the Disputes and the Evidence," *Family Law Quarterly*, 37(2) (2003): 273–301. Retrieved from http://www.jstor.org/stable/25740420
8. We use the term "divorce" to include all types of parenting pairs; for example, parents separated after marriage but not yet divorced, parents who did not marry but lived together, and parents who never married or lived together.

Chapter 2

9. Nicholas Bala, et al., "Parental Alienation: Canadian Court Cases 1989-2008," *Family Court Review*, 48 (2010): 162–177.
10. Demosthenes Lorandos, "Parental Alienation in U.S. Courts, 1985 to 2018." *Family Court Review – Special Issue:* 20/20 on Parent-Child Contact Problems: Concepts, Controversies and Conundrums, Volume 58, No. 2. (April 2020).

Chapter 3

11. Joan Kelly, "Risk and Protective Factors Associated with Child and Adolescent Adjustment Following Separation and Divorce: Social Science Applications," in *Parenting Plan Evaluations: Applied Research for the Family Court*, eds. K. Kuehnle and L. Drozd (New York: Oxford University Press, 2012).
12. Bill Eddy, *Managing High Conflict People in Court* (Scottsdale, AZ: High Conflict Institute Press, 2008).
13. Nancy Collier: https://www.psychologytoday.com/us/blog/inviting-monkey-tea/201503/why-we-hold-grudges-and-how-let-them- go
14. William Fabricius, Sanford Braver, Priscila Diaz, and Clorinda Velez, "Custody and Parenting Time: Links to Family Relationships and Well Being after Divorce," in The Role of the Father in Child Development, 5th ed., ed. M. E. Lamb (Hoboken, NJ: John Wiley & Sons, Inc., 2004).
15. Peggie Ward, "Parent-Child Contact Problems: Alienation and Beyond," Annual Meeting of the Florida Association of Family and Conciliation Courts, September 23, 2019.
16. Robert E. Emery, *Renegotiating Family Relationships: Divorce, Child Custody, and Mediation*, (New York: The Guilford Press, 1994).

Chapter 4

17. Michael Bridges, Transitions: Making Sense of Life's Changes (Cambridge, MA: Da Capo Press, 2003).
18. Joan Kelly, "Risk and Protective Factors Associated with Child and Adolescent Adjustment following Separation and Divorce: Social Science Applications," in Parenting Plan Evaluations: Applied Research for the Family Court, eds. K. Kuehnle and L. Drozd (New York: Oxford University Press, 2012).
19. Judith S. Wallerstein and Sandra Blakeslee, What About the Kids? (New York: Hyperion, 2003).
20. Peter Salem, Irwin Sandler, and Sharlene Wolchik, "Taking Stock of Parent Education in the Family Courts: Envisioning a Public Health Approach," Family Court Review. 51(1), (2013):131–148.
21. Linda Nielsen, "Re-examining the Research on Parental Conflict, Coparenting, and Custody Arrangements," Psychology, Public Policy and Law, 23(2), (2017): 211–231.

Chapter 5

22. Michael Saini, "How Attachment Research and International Peacekeeping Strategies Provide New Hope for Resolution of Intractable Family Conflict and Parent Child Contact Problems," Annual meeting of AFCC, 2019.

23. Guy Burgess and Heidi Burgess, "What are Intractable Conflicts?" Beyond Intractability, Guy Burgess and Heidi Burgess, eds. Conflict Information Consortium. University of Colorado, Boulder. Posted November 2003. http: //www.beyondintractabiity.org/essay/meaning-intractability.

Chapter 6

24. http://mentalfloss.com/article/28434/4-bloody-family-feuds-american-history

25. https://wired.com/2003/06/hatfield-mccoy-truce/

26. The Beyond Intractability Consortium at the University of Colorado under the direction of Guy and Heidi Burgess.

Chapter 7

27. https://en.m.wikibooks.org/wiki/Muggles%27_Guide_to_Harry_Potter/Magic/Dementor

28. Peter Coleman, *The Five Percent: Finding Solutions to Seemingly Impossible Conflicts* (New York: Public Affairs, 2011).

29. Robin Vallacher, et al., "Rethinking Intractable Conflict: The Perspective of Dynamical Systems," *American Psychologist*, 65(4), (2010): 262–278.

30. Melvin R. Lansky, "Forgiveness as the Working Through of Splitting," *Psychoanalytic Inquiry*, 29, (2009): 374–385.

31. Rebecca Bailey et al., "The Application of the Polyvagal Theory to High Conflict Co-parenting Cases," *Family Court Review*, (2020), in press.

Chapter 8

32. Eric Brahm, "Hurting Stalemate Stage," Beyond Intractability. Guy Burgess and Heidi Burgess, eds. Conflict Information Consortium, University of Colorado, Boulder. Posted September 2003.

Chapter 9

33. A Google search for "parenting tips" will yield 3.25 billion results.

Chapter 11

34. Leon Kuczynski, Robyn Pitman, and Kate Twigger, "Flirting with Resistance: Children's Expressions of Autonomy During Middle Childhood," *International Journal of Qualitative Studies on Health and Well-being,* Vol. 13, (2018), https://doi.org/10.1080/17482631.2018.1564519

Chapter 14

35. We strongly encourage the use of online parenting applications to minimize confusion and conflict. Examples of the online coparenting tools are listed in the "Resources" section at the end of this book.

Chapter 15

36. Michelle Maiese, "Limiting Escalation/De-escalation." Beyond Intractability. Guy Burgess and Heidi Burgess, eds. Conflict Information Consortium, University of Colorado, Boulder. Posted January 2004. http://www.beyondintractability.org/essay/limiting-escalation
37. From materials developed for a Neurobiology of Conflict presentation by the Center for Community Dialogue & Training. https://www.ourfamilyservices.org/center/
38. https://www.thecenterforfamilyresolution.com
39. Lois Gold, *Between Love and Hate: A Guide to Civilized Divorce,* (New York: Plume/Penguin, 1992).
40. https://www.psychologytoday.com/us/blog/stronger-the-broken-places/201803/11-tips-conflict-management
41. https://lifehacker.com/how-do-i-get-out-of-an-argument-with-an-irrational-pers-30797995
42. https://www.ccl.org/multimedia/podcast/the-big-6-an-active-listening-skill-set/
43. Bill Eddy, *So What's Your Proposal?: Shifting High-Conflict People from Blaming to Problem-Solving in 30 Seconds!* (Scottsdale AZ: Unhooked Books, LLC, 2014).
44. https://www.psychologytoday.com/us/blog/ulterior-motives/201710/the-growth-mindset-works-not-everyone
45. https://www.stem.org.uk/system/files/community-resources/2016/06/DweckEducationWeek.pdf

Chapter 16

46. Michael Saini, Leslie Drozd, and Robin Deutsch, AFCC Annual Meeting, Toronto, 2019.
47. https://www.psychologytoday.com/us/blog/inviting-monkey-tea/201503/why-we-hold-grudges-and-how-let-them-go
48. The topic of forgiveness is presented in more detail in *Overcoming the Coparenting Trap: Essential Parenting Skills When a Child Resists a Parent* by John Moran, Tyler Sullivan, and Matthew Sullivan, (Overcoming Barriers, Inc., 2015)
49. https://www.pbs.org/kqed/onenight/stories/forgive/index.html

Chapter 17

50. Michael Saini, Janet Johnston, Barbara Fidler, and Nicholas Bala, "Empirical Studies of Alienation," in *Parenting Plan Evaluations: Applied Research for the Family Court*, 2nd ed., eds. Leslie Drozd, Michael Saini, and Nancy Olesen (New York: Oxford University Press, 2016).
51. United Nations Peacekeeping Operations Principles and Guidelines; https://peacekeeping.un.org/sites/default/files/capstone_eng_0.pdf
52. Barbara Fidler, Nicholas Bala, and Michael Saini, *Children Who Resist Post-Separation Parental Contact: A Differential Approach for Legal and Mental Health Professionals*, (New York: Oxford University Press, 2012).
53. Abigail Judge and Robin Deutsch, eds. *Overcoming Parent-Child Contact Problems: Family-Based Interventions for Resistance, Rejection, and Alienation*, (New York: Oxford University Press, 2017).
54. Robin Vallacher et al., "Rethinking Intractable Conflict: The Perspective of Dynamical Systems," *American Psychologist*, 65(4) (2010): 262–278.

COPARENTING RESOURCES

https://afccnet.org/Resource-Center/Resources-for-Families

https://conflictplaybook.com

https://familytransitions-ptw.com/new-beginnings-program/

https://highconflictinstitute.com/on-demand-courses

https://online.divorce-education.com/

https://uptoparents.org

COPARENTING COMMUNICATION TOOLS

https://propercomm.com

https://ourfamilywizard.com

https://talkingparents.com/home

https://coparenter.com

https://civilcommunicator.com

https://www.cozi.com

https://sharekids.com

MEDIA

https://amazon.ca/Welcome-Back-Pluto-Understanding-Preventing/dp/B0042QDAQ4

Made in the USA
Monee, IL
14 January 2021